*Di*eagnosis

by
VOTH

Dieagnosis

by
VOTH

RIOT OF ROSES
PUBLISHING HOUSE
SEJATNGA
UNCEDED TONGVA TERRITORY
SOUTH WHITTIER, CALIFORNIA

Published by Riot of Roses Publishing House

Dieagnosis
© 2023, Gabriel Acosta
ISBN: 978-1-961717-05-3 (paperback)
ISBN: 978-1-961717-06-0 (ebook)
Library of Congress Control Number: 9781961717053

First Edition, 2023

To request permissions, you may contact the Publisher at riotofrosesllc@gmail.com

Printed in the United States of America

www.riotofrosespublishinghouse.com

Edited by Brenda Vaca
Cover Design by Jim Dodson
Layout Design by Krystle May Statler

In memory of Brenda Lee Acosta,
my favorite person and heroine.

She was the first person to honor and welcome my differences, and
she encouraged me to be who I am without fear.

August 16, 1967–December 11, 2020

Table of Contents

Chapter II: Evaluation: A.R.T.

Chapter III: Consultation: Blinded by Darkness

Chapter IV: *Die*agnosis: Faces of Evil

Chapter V: Treatment

Foreword

I first met VOTH in 2021 when I was fresh in my first year of teaching poetry. That year was full of challenges for me as I had just released my own book that I couldn't promote, I was struggling to manage my own mental health in the middle of the COVID pandemic, and I was going through depressive episodes. The first time VOTH read one of his poems during workshop, I was in awe of his raw perspective on life and I couldn't help but to reflect on my own journey in life and as a poet. Our stories intertwined in our intersectionalities as queer/gay kids and now adults. Here was a poet in full transparency sharing his story to a Zoom room of strangers. In between the praises and feedback, VOTH was often unaware of how his work truly impacted me as the instructor, but also how his poems added to the growth of the class. Every workshopped poem was a performance and I knew that VOTH was ready to start hitting the stages with his work to begin impacting audiences all over Los Angeles. But we were quarantined, and IG live streams became stages, Zoom rooms offered healing to a grieving community, and VOTH had yet to discover his own power as a writer and poet.

Toward the end of the semester, he stopped showing up to class, so I wrote him an email telling him how much his work needed to be heard. I urged him to return the next semester and shared how important it was that he finish his book so that he could share it with the community. He returned the next semester and finished this collection of poems, where he shares overcoming some of the most difficult times in his life. From his medical diagnosis to suicidal ideation, VOTH allows the reader to enter intimate places of affliction, regret, and unhappiness. Every word was a piercing blade and each poem, a reflection of intimate and personal experiences that have made him stronger and more visible in his search to heal his body, mind, and soul. The poems are honest and come from dark places that most of us fear to go to. His journey provides hope and inspiration, as he shows that it is possible to overcome even the most difficult obstacles by practicing self-reflection and self-love. His poems allow permission to share the messy, tragic, and traumatic parts of life unapologetically and without filters.

VOTH's poems are a powerful testament to the strength of the human spirit and this collection of poems shows that it is possible to find oneself in the midst of chaos. Queer kids and adults often have to rise out of the ashes no matter how many times we burn. VOTH's rebirth from these experiences is revolutionary and is a reminder that we don't exist alone in these moments. I hope that this collection of poems will inspire the reader to keep moving through the discomfort in order to get to the pleasurable parts of life. Our journeys aren't linear and we must allow ourselves grace in between the blows. Trauma does not have to define us. With time, support, and self-compassion, we can learn to cope with our suffering and live our lives to the fullest.

—Andrés Sánchez, Author of *This Body*

Exordium

Hello Beautiful Souls,

Dieagnosis is the journey of my life from the age of thirteen (2007) to the age of twenty-eight (2022). The poems you are about to journey through tell my story, my vulnerability, and my truth. Countless wars of "who I am" and "where am I going" have helped me discover and answer questions I've asked myself for years. Every diagnosis has had a tremendous effect on my life from nearly giving up to no longer wanting to exist to wanting to live. The ups and downs to hitting rock bottom. Then to be welcomed by Death again and **choosing** to fight.

It has been an extraordinary adventure. So many times I wanted to give up, but I got back up and kept going. This beautiful life we live is an adventure and wherever you're at in yours, the worst possible outcome won't always be the case. I urge you to **please keep going.**

For this collection, I have a workbook titled *Beacon*. The introduction of the workbook is to remind yourself of who you are, what your dreams are, what you hope for, and what you desire most in life. The "meat" of the workbook is about healing trauma – a safe space of self-expression. In *Beacon*, there are activities, writing prompts, affirmations, and tools to help navigate you to find *you*. This workbook will remind you that in order to be mentally free, you have to build a routine of self-care. Begin the great adventure of traveling inward to rediscover who you are by healing trauma.

Feel comfortable. Be you. Respect who you are and how you feel. You are valid.

Throughout this journey you will come across important pages called Checkpoints, Intros, Notes, and Outro.

Checkpoints: to signify interaction with you and hold space.

Intros: written to signify the blood of my body. They are introductions to each chapter.

Notes: short poems representing whispers of hope and strength to keep going. They are the "I can do this."

Outro: written to signify oxygen. In Chapter 5 *Treatment,* I was healing trauma. At the end of writing the chapter, breathing felt differently. Breathing for my body, breathing for my mind, and breathing for my soul. I was finally able to take a breath, pause, and feel closer to life.

I would love to hear your voice and/or read about who you are. Break open the pen and allow the ink to share your story. Tag me on Instagram @voth_94_

Collect your thoughts through breath for positivity. Remain patient for your long-term desires. Be persistent for your short-term hopes. If something is at your fingertips, reach out just a little more, take the next step and embrace all of it. Learn your loophole and break the cycle. The "pit" doesn't have to last forever. Climb out of the grave and take your power back. Become a beacon.

Love and Light,

VOTH | Voice of the Harbor

P.S. Please take a moment to step back and take a breath as needed.

Flip the page and let us begin our journey.

Chapter I
History

Intro 1

Growing up,
    darkness was all I knew.

It shaped my soul.

Devoured my life essence,
and soon became a part of me
like a parasitic teratoma
that would take over.

Breaking free each time,
is a war for control.

Maybe,
    I just…
            I have to…
    Give in…

Plague

I want to escape
but the dark thoughts
tantalize
      my humanity.
      My soul
      will never be
      set free.

I just need a moment-
      a second to breathe.

I'm in a battle for freedom,
yet I'm crippled and shackled
in my own mental asylum.

Mirror | rorriM

I wish I saw you,

the way I see you now.

Then, was so complicated,
and now it is much different.

I am more confident
in everything I do,
and I owe it all to

You.

Love's Shadow

My body is filled with a broken heart.
Every day I begin to gain
so much pain.

I used to visit the meadows
where I felt safe and could be me.
Now, I'm in the shadows,
locked up, and I threw away the key.

It feels like I'm in a game
where the goal is non-existent.
Everything is the same
like a toxic loophole of conviction.

While in the meadows
I felt safe and could be me,
but now I'm in the shadows,
locked up, and I threw away the key.

Someone show me where my path truly lies.
There is so much loss in my eyes.

Here in the meadows,
I am plagued by a shadow
who looks just like me
and he is taunting me with a key.

Cursed!

When you're in a mess
you don't think it can get *any* worse.
Feels like the blessed
become executed with a brilliant curse.

When it happens to someone else
it's,
>   *"I'm so sorry. How can I help?"*
But when it happens to you, they say,
>   *"How sad."*
>   They say,
>   *"Poor thing."*

It hurts to remember
the loss and the pain.
I wish it was December.
The gifts, fun, snow, and rain.

"Everything happens for a reason"

sounds like a shitty pick-up line.
The requiem for a new season
has come and will redefine
my truth.

Love's Fear

Love is sometimes
like a mysterious growth.
We don't always understand it
and when we try, we can't breathe.

As long as you are alive,
it'll continue its development.
When people hug and kiss you,
they say,
>   *"I love you."*

The feeling in my chest
makes my eyes watery
because I'll never
get to love *him* in person.

Loving him is Gay,
but what does that truly mean?

Christ-is

I hate it when she screams;
        the disapproving voice of my
            mother.

The blaring cry triggers my hand
to reach   for the black hilt.

Sometimes I want to stand
at a corner
like the Strawberries of Compton.

What's worse?

My trigger-happy hand
        or being bent over in a dirty, smelly alley?

I dislike this life.
I do, but don't want another.
As I reach   for the sterling silver blade,
my conscience says,
        "Don't bother."

I can't do it again.

It's too hard to contemplate
my death and my existence.

At the school yard,
my wounds cry for the grave
as my soul weeps for deliverance.

All I did was like a boy
and now they punish me
for my sin.

Chanting verses and psalms
to make me feel guilty.
Stoning me to save my soul
instead of loving and accepting my

     Truth.

Walking down the church hall,
       will I be denied?

Catch me as I
         f
         a
         l
         l.

Cristo!
     My suicide.

I Am

I am different and strange.
I wonder if there is more than I can see.
I hear the cries of the innocents.
I see world peace.
I am different and strange.

I pretend to be someone I'm not.
I feel the pain of those who isolate.
I touch those who are in pain.
I worry about the ones I'm not near.
I cry of the pain that no one can see.
I am different and strange.

I understand why things happen in life.
I say that everything happens for a reason.
I dream of love and happiness.
I try to make those I can happy.
I hope for hate and suffering to stop.
I am different and strange.

Have You Truly Seen Me?

From far and wide
take your life
and cast it aside.

Control yourself.
Remember the dream.
The life you wanted.
You still have time to redeem.

Don't turn away.
You still have time.
Don't close your eyes.
Just follow the rhyme.

If you're feeling stuck
change the route.
If you need to cry,
let the pain out.

Repress your fears
or you'll drown
in a madness of tears.

Talk to me.
I'm standing right here.
I'm not like others
in the atmosphere.

You're not a ghost.
You can be seen.
You already know
that I'm not mean.

Voices of the wind.
Sounds of the sea.
You now know
everything about me.

Escaped

I'm trying to escape
the sound of screams.
Looking up towards the dark sky
and see illuminated beams.

The bright light
staring down at me
vanishes from my sight,

leaving me in the dark once more.
I feel cold chills
flowing throughout my core.

I can't breathe.
No matter how hard I try.

Beginning to regain control
of an involuntary action,
but I feel as if my worlds
are about to shift and collide.

There is so much sorrow
in my eyes and I'm blind.
Show me where my path lies
so I can be free

from this madness.
My mind has sparked.
I don't want to live in this sadness,
so I have marked

the answer I've been seeking.
Feeling it through my body.

Lurking through my veins
like it's some odd disease.
One day this pain will cease.

to exist from my world.
From the kingdom high above
comes the Lord.

My soul so black
has turned white,
so no longer will I lack
with a soul so black.

Lost...

I'm in the world
alone and lost.
The first frost
has encased my body.

Freezing nights go by.
Everything in sight vanished.
All of the choices I've made
have been forgotten and slayed.

Misery's bitterness has left me
to decide.
Another desire has failed
and died.

My dream is real and here.
All I've done is hide in fear.

Lost...
Lost...
Lost...

Wait!

I see the light, shining ever so bright.
Showing me the way to a better life

than to stay in a world so black.
The star has made a crack
in the brilliant dark sky—

a crack so huge that it is now day.
The sun shines its
magnificent, majestic rays.

Born from fear,
I see a rope without
a destination.

I WILL CLIMB.

How Do You Know?

My brain keeps
questioning my love
for you,
        my mother.

You can't possibly know
my life.

You keep telling me,
        "I've been there,
                I've done that,
        so I know."

You don't know anything!

You don't know what it's like
to look in the mirror and see
NOTHING!

I try my best to please you.

You're in the background
parading my mistakes
instead of acknowledging
my accomplishments.

You say that
        I'm lazy.
                I drive you crazy.

You're my mom,
and I'm trying my best
to change.

Changing is a process,
not an overnight transition.

Riddled in the outdated line:
    "I know."

        But dear mother, to truly know
        is to truly understand the gift
        of the unknown.

You don't know what it's like:
        to BLEED from your wrists
        to HIDE from the public eye
        to EXPOSE and claim your identity
        to COME OUT and say
        I'm GAY.

Then to watch the world
around you collapse
like a domino effect
from HELL.

So, please tell me mother,
how could you possibly
        know?

Blood and Stones

When you stare at the ground
and gaze upon the stones around,

never do you wonder,
how many bones they crushed?

How many times they've been
chucked?

Ripping through the air
and bashing a head or a limb.

You never know the damage
until you stare at them:
          discolored.

Some are brown and shocked.
Others are painted by nature,
but there's always that one
with a bloody reminiscence
          of an *untold* truth.

Dream Slave

I'm so tired of feeling
lost in a dream I can't escape from.
Trying to wake up every day,
yet I continue to be a slave

in a world where only
broken hearts exist.

I'm like ice.
Not transparent though

solid.

      Fragile.

I've been dropped and I

    S   H

      A   T

              T

                 E

                    R

                 E   D

Rebuilding myself brick by brick,
clay, and metal until I am armor.

Shake me! Wake me!
From this evil dream.

Shake me! Wake me!
From this loveless place.

Shake me! Wake me!
From this loveless dream.
Shake me! Wake me!
From this evil place.

Memory

I hold a memory I can't speak.
A haunting memory that triggers
the darkest parts of my thoughts.

Memory, I banish thee
from the corners of my mind.

Closing my eyes,
   I see you,
      watch you
         cause pain.

I open my eyes
   and I don't see you,
   but I feel a sharp burn
      coming from my veins.

Small of mind, big of woe.
The suffering you caused,
   you now will know.

Love, Gabriel

Many LGBTQ+ Youth are homeless.

The world is a scary place.
Growing up we were afraid of the closet,
and knew not to look under the bed.
We were skeptical of baths,
and curious how blue veins turned red
when we bled.

The world is a peculiar place.
Growing up we were afraid to come out of the closet,
and when scared hid under our beds.
We loved to take baths with sorted shampoos,
and still wondered why we bled red.

The world is an unknown place.
We are out of the closet but now I'm all alone,
and the only place I can call home is a mattress,
in a box, and on the side of the street.
We loved to take baths with fragrant shampoos,
but now I'm like a cat licking my wounds.

The world is a knowledgeable place.
I know why we bleed red. When the burning
sweet oxygen meets our blood it changes color,
but also the light penetrating our skin illuminates the flesh
underneath to appear like another.

I wanted to be a doctor,
but I'll be known as the Boy who shamed his parents. The Boy who
spent hours in his closet contemplating life and existence. The
Boy who became homeless in a matter of days. The Boy who was
wrapped in sheets and who was found dead.

The world is a tragic place.
If I make the news, they'll find this letter.
They'll know my story, but not the plot
twists, the climax, the "Oh my God."
The part that makes your stomach knot.

When goosebumps flood
your skin like some odd disease.
When the hairs on your body
rise involuntarily.
When the mother abandoned her son
because God told her to.

When the father swings
without hesitation because it's not
what he views.

When the world he knew turned away,
because the only truth he kept secret
was that he was **Gay.**

Pill Bottle

I've made a terrible mistake.
I slipped down some pills
with a Hennessy Milkshake.

Walking to my bedroom
pill bottle in hand.
Stumbling over my feet,
feeling queasy.

All of the other kids,
they wouldn't care.
I'm the black sheep,
the ghost, the shadow
      in the corner.

      "You are more.
            So much more."

I must stop ignoring my life.
If I am to make it to tomorrow
I must end this tragedy.

      All that I'm living for will not,
      will not be ended by a cryptic knife
      with an entree of cough syrup
      and a side of ecstasy.

Your glow is so hypnotic.
       Enchanting.
              Inviting.
                     Holy.
              Radiant.
       Are you an
angel or are you the devil?

Calling

Watching a body rise to the sky.
The heavens have called you.

Our sweet angel,
your time has come.
Leave the ties that bind you
and it shall be done.

Do not dwell upon us
You must go now.
We set you free.

> Guardian Angel,
> give my sister guidance and company.
> Do not leave her side.
> Protect her always.
> Return her now
> from whence she came.
> From time and space
> we let you depart this place.

Today, we bless the memories
we hold dearly.
We cherish them with kindness
and never with blind acts of fear.

Blessed be.

Vampires

Lurking through the night
        but not during the day.
In this dark hour
        they come out to play.

Roaming from city to city
        in packs or rogue.
These heartless creatures
        will rip you apart.

Smelling you from miles away
like a fine wine dine buttered fillet.

They want a party: a feast.
You're their flesh to suck into.
Their Friday night rare prime steak.
A special juice box of

juicy crimson red
        blood.

Open Door: A Conversation with a Friend

You can't go.
You can't leave.

I know that life
          doesn't always have an
                    answer.
But the more you push
life will cease to suck.

Before I met you,
I was beyond hope.
While beside you,
I was alive.

Dwelling in the shadows
          away from the light.
Behind the door
          that hides you tonight.

Don't shed another tear.
I'm right here and
I'll never leave.

Open the door.
Put the scissors down!
Look in the mirror!

The possessive mask
isn't you. It's pseudo.

She drops the crossing blades
and lets me in.

Nightmares and Lost Dreams: Darkness

When I was alone,
I found comfort in the darkness.
When I was sad,
I found comfort in the shadows.

They welcomed me with open arms.

My blood became black.
My mind was hidden amongst fear.
My heart turned cold and
my soul was tainted
   in everlasting darkness.

My Darkness

My darkness isn't up for conversation.
Isn't said during drinks or used as an icebreaker.
My darkness wasn't and isn't a joke.

Do you think I laughed when the glass
broke my skin?
Do you think I smiled when the paperclip
lifted away my cells and drew blood?

The first time I was in a police car
>I wanted to die.
>I wanted to die for reasons
>I didn't understand.

I wanted to become the ghost

I had already **become.**

Broken

Years of war and a life of pain.
A mystical dark core
engraved into my brain.

Goddess, please help me,
I'm living with a shackled soul.

I've lived a cowardly life.
Letting bullies dissect
and rearrange my light.

5th grade Suicide.
6th grade Deadly Pack.
7th grade Traumatize.
8th grade Attack.

Falling to pieces
        for what I am.

        Gay.

Strange how this word
controlled my way of life.
How the homophobic
would taunt me,
        degrade me,
                ambush me.

I became their prey.
        Like a coven of vampires,
                they tortured me and
        out of fear, I allowed them
to feast on me.

Together we can change.
We shouldn't be ashamed.

Together, we can change.
We shouldn't be ashamed.
to accept ourselves
            for who we are.

Our voice can suture
            not the past
but the future to give
            the next generation
                        a chance.

So they can live
            a peaceful life
with a touch of tranquility
            and clarity.

My journey is the beginning
            and my story
                        shall never
            End.

You
   changed
my
   world,
but
   you
also
   took
my
   heart.

Nightmares and Lost Dreams: Nightmare

Lost in the streets of the living
is where one is supposed to find home,
but as I begin to lurk these crooked alleys
my heart and soul, mind and body, begin to fade.

The passion to disappear has come once more.
If I go, I'll no longer be hostile to anyone.

"An abomination of demonic fury,"
            —that's what I've been titled.

A turbulent sinister evil; the *cursed* one.

"Conclude his life.
            Terminate his destiny."

Disappearance

Having me write something joyful
is like forcing me to breathe.
My life has hit a turning point
and telling me to leave.

I know my life is good
but the way I see it
it's a cryptic code of
lifeless wit.

I know you're going to say,
        "What are you talking about?
        Your life hasn't even begun."
Yet, all I hear are whispers and doubt.

I tell my father that I have to go
to the doctor's.
My back is in pain, but all he says,
        "You're insane."

Lub, dub. Lub, dub.
Lub, dub. Lub, dub.

Thy hatred has come
along with the horses of doom.

My mother, she says,
        "You're so dramatic."

Watching as I stand and ache.
Live and love is just a phrase.
My future is at stake
and I'm trapped in a maze.

The man I want to become
is at a distance.
Darkened beams strike
the tug-of-war resistance.

I'm losing my mind.
The clock's ti-ti-ti-ticking
has come to a halt
as the memories flicker.

My journey is near its end.
Shall I go, or will I stay?
Space can no longer bend
the fabric of time.

Onward, into the light
from this perilous dark night,
I will **evolve**.

Un*known* Harm

My blood pressure rises
At the sound of your voice.
It decreases when you're not
      around.

Your absence relieves the
tension.
Going to the doctor
seems to get your attention.

Outbursts of our family
coming from every direction.

How many more outbursts
      until I crack?

When will you get it?
When will you believe me?

When will you get
that I've built a tolerance
      to live?

You fail to see the symptoms
growing within my exhausted body.

I smell the metallic iron of blood.
I taste its frequency in my throat.
My head sings the song of madness.
The pulsating blood blinds my sight.

You helped manifest this tragic horror
ripping through my mind,
and you did so
      un*knowing*ly.

We live
in the land
of the living
where no one
understands
how we
feel.

When I close my eyes,
I see what should never be shown.
When I close my eyes,
I ascend into a world unknown.

Night Terror

At night,
half of us lie
awake, wide-eyed,

afraid of the nightmares
that haunt us,
while others fall
fast asleep.

Some nightmares are just
        dreams.
Others are real.

Deep in our minds
lie the secrets
we're afraid to speak.

Our minds spin
around,
        and around,
and around.

Unmasking the reality
of the truth.

It's not what we see;
we're blind.
It's not what we hear;
we're deaf.

The tears that scald,
our skin is what we fear,
because then reality becomes clear
to the chattering audience.

I had a dream.

Such a beautifully...

delicious dream.

Dear Passenger,

This is a checkpoint.
Stand up.
Stretch.
Take a break.

Be mindful of how you respect your body.
Drink some water.
Your kidneys and skin will be happy.

Be mindful of how you respect your mind.
Give yourself space to breathe and scream.
Acknowledge when you are upset.

Be mindful of how you respect your spirit.
Trauma can twist who you are.
Acknowledge what you need.

Chapter II
Evaluation: A.R.T.

Intro 2

In the chapter I'm about to share, I was inflicted by a malevolent darkness. I expressed this new rage with a few words and a lovely red flower. As nightfall would take over, so did my power. Rampage echoed through their minds and the truth forced *them* to be blind.

Once Upon a Nightmare

Once upon a nightmare,
I was lost and alone.
Everyone would stare.
I didn't have a home.
Through my eyes white was black,
and black was void.
My heart was metallic;
android.
When I closed my eyes to sleep,
I was consumed by eternal darkness.
Marked by fear I would weep
until I was met by darkness once more.
The entity of all and nothing;
everything and anything.
All I craved
was true happiness,
but for those of us who crave it,
we will always starve.

My Sweet Annihilation

R

T

Asylum

Trapped in a room
with nowhere to go.
The doors are locked
and the windows are stone.
Clawing at the floor
but it doesn't make a dent.
My hands are sore and
my back is always bent.
Praying up to the Lord
to let me be free
of this nightmare I've endured
for the past ten years I think it
       will be.
You'll never know
the feeling 'till it happens.
The fear inside will grow and
for a while all you'll be doing is laughin'.
Laughing away the insanity,
depriving yourself of sleep.
There is no room for sanity.
Only the darkness that deeply creeps.
Trapped in the four walls
of a troubled teen.
Lost in all the brawls
I was seen.
Living in the room
for the insane.
My life has been a joyous sin.
Can you think of no one to blame?
The only light is a candle.
Shall it go out?
Then, so shall I...

Insanity

It hurts to lose the ones you love.
Ripped away from who matters most.
No matter how deep you bury the past,
it will always haunt you.

> *"Don't look back because*
> *time is running out.*
> *Keep moving forward because*
> *you need to find a way out."*

Dwelling
in the back
      of your mind.
Trying
to push it
          away.
It fights back.
Losing yourself one too many times.
When do we stop the fear?

> *"You don't. Just accept it."*

I am beginning to become
      someone
         Else.

MuTaTiOn

I have changed.
I feel like a monster.
Something is gone.
Something feels wrong.
There's a war in my head.
The battle continues to grow.

I feel weak, yet powerful.

The transformation
paralyzes my thoughts.
The freezer burn
crystallizes my heart.

Am I a Villain?

My thoughts are not mine.

My brain is fried.
I'm like a modern day Frankenstein.
Something within has died.
I have been modified.

After all of these lies,
the rage continues to grow.

Have I become a Monster?

This war in my head
has spread throughout
my body. I can't hear anything
except for my blaring cries.

My thoughts are paralyzed.
My flesh is burning away.
My heart has crystallized.
I am now a bouquet of decay.

Sound of Death

Boom, boom. Boom, boom.
This strange sound follows me.
It makes two quick beats
and then pauses.
Repeats.
Boom, boom. Boom, boom.
Haunts me.
Boom, boom. Boom, boom.
Disturbs me when I wake.
Boom, boom. Boom, boom.
As I slumber.
   Why doesn't this sound disappear?
 Boom, boom. Boom, boom.
   Why must it lurk at every corner?
 Boom, boom. Boom, boom.
It gets louder when I
   run.
 Boom, boom. Boom, boom.
Slows down when I lie
   still.
Boom, boom. Boom, boom.
A new sound emerged
  as I slumbered deep.
Beeeeeeeep...

Limbo

Whenever the wind blows,
I begin to pray.
Has my time come?
Have I become the prey?
Running through time
as if it doesn't even matter.
Not stopping to dine
otherwise I'll get even fatter.
Timeline of depression.
King of the joust.
When's the time of repression?
Peasants have been housed.
Who's our savior?
We need a hero!
Children in labor!
Goodbye Pharaoh!
Ave Maria,
where did you go?
Help me return
to kingdom come.
Lord Almighty,
how did you know?
How did you leave
this prison I call Hell?
Help me!
   Help me!
Help me!
   Help me!
Every movement
has been amplified
to one million.
Sounds of recompression
blow your mind
to one billion.

¡Ayúdame!
      ¡Ayúdame!
¡Ayúdame!
      ¡Ayúdame!
Ave Maria,
Lord Almighty,
Help me return
to kingdom come.
Ave Maria,
Lord Almighty,
help me escape
the gates of Hell.
Lord Almighty,
Ave Maria!
Help me return
to the gates of Heaven.
Help me escape
this darkened void.
Ayuda me, help me!
      Ayuda me, help me!
Ayuda me, help me!
      Ayuda me, help me!
Whenever the wind blows
I begin to creep to
Limbo.

Lost Words

Misguided words
can cause so much
      damage.
Words, they flow through the wind
passing a message.
Messages are lost all of the time.
Never able to be retrieved by
      the recipient.
Lost words and endless silence.
Broken songs and restless violence.
The lyrics of the *golden* pages
have been forgotten.
The words of the living
are now *dead*.
Just **listen**.
Listen to the wind.
      Listen to the beating hearts.
Become sound.
      Become the rhythm.
Hear the frequency.
Listen to the wind.
Hear the words
      flow through your
mind.
Listen to the wind.
Hear the message
      of the Gods.
Listen for your
      future.
Listen to the wind.
Listen to your surroundings.
      Listen with your voice.
Listen with your eyes.

Listen with your mind.
Smell the words.
     Taste the endless silence.
Touch the forgotten.
     Bring them to life.
Guided spirits, hear my plea.
Return the cords of my voice
to speak the words of the truth.
So mote it be.
Misguided words of tomorrow
     shall be remembered once more.

A

Resurrection of a Dark Soul

T

Forgive Me

Infinite times a day,
I had to risk my own pain
to save a stranger's life.

It was the hardship of
      self-sacrifice.

To let go of the emotional bonds
you worked so hard to create.
The tear in your heart
will only widen.

Humans dream. We redeem
ourselves when we're ready
to release the darkness within.

Fear is:

      Frequent echoes alternating rest.
           or
      Freedom evoking abundant radiance.

It's so loud inside my head
with words I should have never said.
I drown in my own regret.

We never saw eye-to-eye.
So, it always seemed one
was telling a lie.

Even though it's so loud in my head
I've balanced out the actions
with the words I should have never said.

I will no longer drown in my own regret.
So, I alone will rise and face the threat,
but first,

I forgive you.

For the first time in a long time,
the screaming in my head
disappears.
The pain grows as it repairs.

Infinite times a day
I have to risk my own pain
to save a stranger's life.

Forgive me.

It is the hardship of
self-sacrifice.

Incarcerated Instrument

I am a robot.
Reprogrammed.
Doing what the haunting voices say.

In the corner, I rust.

I am a puppet.
Ligaments being controlled.

I had freedom.
Once again I've been caged.

Voices pick through my brain.
Stripping pieces away like a mad scientist.

I am human, yet, as I'm trying to run I am pulled back.
Am I huma-a-an?
My thoughts are not my own.

Am I not truly alive?

I can't breathe.
You're always at my side.
I, for a change, want to know what it's like
to have trust, faith, and hope that I can do things on my own.

Since I was a young bo-o-ot,
you've always been there.
I want nothing more than to not feel scared.
Yet again, I am disappointing not you, but myself.

I am huma-a-an.

I want to know what it's like
to not be denied
a life I've dreamt
since surviving suicide.

I want to be happy-y-y,
yet as I preach, as I vent,
my circuits override.

I am denied

the freedom I've longed for deep inside.

I a-a-am.

I…

Forgotten Shadow

In the shadows
is where I once felt safe.
Now that I'm standing in the light,
it burns.

My once iced heart
is now beating and warm.
The air we breathe is filled
with lies and deception.

Who are you now
that your brain has followed
a false education?

I can only presume
there will be no salutation.
Between I and the Jury,
I am now an abomination.

Beyond their eyes
there is confusion.

If I am not a brother,
if you are not a sister,
then who are we now?

Who are *we* now?

      Strangers?

Faceless wonder
of an assumed expectation.

We are family,
yet you deny our shared blood.

If I am not your brother,
then I am now nothing
but a forgotten shadow.

In the darkness
is where I felt safe.
But now that I'm standing
in the light...
It burns.

Celestial

My mind is a fool and led me to believe
that I was lesser than a human being.

My mind changes in the night
and nights before a full moon.

Is it not real?

Am I greater or lesser than
what I've sought my entire life?
And if I am who they say I am
then why do I still feel different?

Fog rolls in and fog rolls out,
yet I still hear the cries of lost souls.

If I am human
then why do I hear
the man with a skull face
dressed in black?

Why do I see shadows dancing
in your head?

If they're not really there
then why do you and I,
I and the world feel scared?

When I dream, my body floats,
so where do you think it goes?

Where does it go?

If not within our heads
then a place of lost goals?

The darkness keeps reminding me
of what I lost inside.

The body I walk in has no self-control.

I see what's in your head.
You're afraid of the unknown.
But you're human,
afraid of what can't be seen.

So, as I lie here under the stars,
I stare into the eyes of the moon.
Hearing the whispers of those around
and thoughts of broken sound.

The night is my friend
and I am its Guardian.

Forward from the Past

If I gave it my all
I never would have lost you.

You were always there
when I needed a friend.

I can hear your soul calling me.

       I don't want to see it.

I don't want to touch it.

I don't want to keep waiting
for your voice to call mine.

Best of us goes down.

I'm holding back
the thrashing river.
It's almost a year since
I've taken shelter.

All I can do is wait.

I had to go to church
to open the floodgates.

Say you love me.

I still have high hopes.
Even if it takes years and years.

I don't want another love.

I'll stand here and wait.
I'll stand here and breathe.

I've fallen short, but I'll be good.

If I gave it my all
I wouldn't be losing you.

I don't want to see it.

      I don't want to feel it.

I don't want to open the oceans.

      I have waited for you to call me.

It feels like I've waited years.

I must journey for love because
the love of my youth is falling short.

Sitting in my shelter,
the thrashing river has begun to fall.

I cannot wait for you to call my name.

      I can't wait.

I have found myself
in a field of lost dreams
beside your soul.

Let our souls
find peace together.
Lean on and let us soar
to a place I've dreamt of once before

I had to go to church
to open the oceans.

I'm glad I did so.

Forgiven but Never Forgotten...

Infinite times a day
the world is screaming in decay.
I have to risk my own pain
to save others from disdain.

I broke the ties because spies
in their eyes filled their head with lies.
I could not afford another surprise.
Waiting would be unwise.

So, I alone severed the bond
to reclaim those who would respond.
Over time I grew very fond
of their existence; we correspond.

One day, another will spawn
and I will be ready in the waking
of that dawn.

I hope one day
without the need of foul play,
we can all move forward with our lives.
Those who don't may be deprived.

The tear in my heart
has sealed once more.
Hopefully we can move to a fresh start.
Maybe even restore

what was lost in the fire.
But if not, we can always soar higher.

I've released the darkness
from beyond within.

I've suppressed all of my stress
lying underneath my skin.

Hope is:

> Haunting obsessions patronize egos.
>   or
> Healing offers positive evolution.

It's so quiet inside of my head
ever since I laid the pain to rest.

I rise content
and words which will be
heard and said.

My new actions will save lives.

The choices I make redefine.

I see the world with new found eyes.
I must be honest. I must be brave.
I will surprise the unwise.
I will reprise myself and save the ignored
        "slaves."

The quiet in my head
is beginning to scream and shout.

> *Just listen!*

Listen to my words.
        Hear with your heart.
Listen to the dying world.
        Do your part.

I will rise and face the threat.
I will no longer drown in my own regret.

For too long I have denied
the pride I carry deep inside.
I must continue to guide
the lost and denied.

Breaking the walls,
      the barriers from inside.

My hopes, my dreams, my goals will provide
me with the supplies on the other side.

Infinite times a day
the world's people are the prey.

I must risk my own pain
to free them of their
      "chains and broken reign."

I hope one day I will be forgiven,
      but never will I be forgotten.

A
R The evolution of a beautiful
Transformation

We Are One HumanITY (I Trusted You)

We...
We are...
We are one.

I can hear their footsteps coming.
I hear their voices scream.
I can hear them getting closer.
They are coming for me.

Why are we so unbalanced?
Can't they see we're all the same?

They think I'm poisonous.
They think Gays are to blame.

We are one.
But the world is dysfunctional.

We are one.
What are we to become?

We are one.
But they don't seem to care.

Everyone wants a role
in this infinite war.

I fear the day when I travel,
I'll be surrounded like a pig knowingly
waiting to be slain.

We are human.

Where's your humanity?
I trusted you!

We...
We are...
We are one!

I stood by your side.
We never had to hide.
They assumed I lied.
You'll never know how much
 I died inside.

We are only human and
I trusted you.

I fought.
I battled.
I lost warriors.
I survived.

I am so cold
all of the time.
I have so much emotion
for a passenger of life.

We are one.
I trusted you.

We are one
and I trusted you.

This is the aftermath
of the war.

I would be lying
if I got down on my knees
and said,

"I'm tired of trying."

We...
We are...
We are one human—
I
Trusted
You.

Human

Shattered around,
you'll discover millions of pieces of stone.
But on the ground
you'll realize it's heart and bone.

Humans break.
We discover and make.
We cry and we weep.
We say things from our sleep.

But if you don't hear it from me
then why believe it?

I have fallen and I've failed
but I have not flailed.
I've made my wrongs right
but they believe I've lost sight.

You think you know me,
yet you have no idea who I am.
Why are you so blind to see
I am not an ordinary man?

I'm not perfect
but neither are you.

I am just human,
just like you.

Human.

But if you don't hear it from me then why believe it?

Don't come to me
with your opinions.
Convince me
with your evidence.

I am not perfect,
nor are you.

I am just human,
just like you.

Human.

Shattered around,
you will find me on the ground
lifting myself from this tragic place,
and into the hands of grace.

Who Am I?

I am the HEALER
of the lost and forgotten.

I see beyond the naked eye.
I am a GUARDIAN:
a raven of vision.

I am the burning FLAME
dancing gracefully through
your candlewick.

I will
forever be the LIGHT
to your darkness.

So,
when you need me
just WHISPER.

I'll hear your CALL.

Forbidden Temptation

I feel it, feel it in my mind.
I feel it, feel it coursing through my drive.
I don't know how to get it out of my head.
Don't know how I will survive.

Black cherries are my sublime.
They keep me from this seductive crime.
If it's not released,
I will never live in peace.

I see it, see it, it's in my view.
The tasteful sight is pumping through.
If I don't become blind soon,
I'll do something to be accused.

Walking through the meadow
of a corpsed heart.
I can feel the rays of a shadow
within thy broken art.

The colors pasted on
its raptured skin
fuels my body with
nothing but sin.

Oh I can't handle myself;
it's too close to my palms.
I can't see clearly
for my path is blurry.

Surrounded by
a ravenous bliss.
I can't seem to awaken
from this maleficent kiss.

It feeds through
my every being
trying to take control and
possess me.

This toxic lust
will not get through,
for I have a field of strawberries
to keep me due.

If they can't keep
my hormones down,
then I don't know
what will become of the town.

I taste it, taste it, it's on my tongue.
The taste of blood is like a drug.
Once you taste it you can't get enough,
but thank god for their legs because I like it when they

RUN!

I heard it, heard it from afar.
Their cries muffled through the burning car.
I took one last look before I fled.
That's when darkness sat comfortably in my head.

Hold on. (I can't let it break free)
Hold on. (Have faith)
Hold on. (I am a Guardian)
Hold on. (This temptation is wrong)

I smell it, smell it, it is strong.
The poison has reached my core.
I can't keep living life this way.
I must shut this God damn destructive door and

feel it
see it
taste it
hear it
smell it

No more.

noitcelfeR | Reflection

I was so sure
but then I saw the truth.
Nobody is perfect
and neither are you.

When I see the light,
I see your face.
When I look into the mirror,
I see your pain.

All the sacrifices
you had to make.
With only pain gained,
transformed into black stains.

But these stains
shall not flow
throughout my veins
for my strength shall always grow.

My strength shall always grow!

I always thought
you should know.
You can't understand the known
until you experience the unknown.

When the sky transforms into night,
I can feel your body and your spirit intensify.
With nothing but sorrow you've always had might.

Your illuminating identity
will always petrify my every being.
No one will ever justify again
who I am supposed to be.

My light will always magnify
and shine over those who dare
to utilize me
for their unfair wrongful song.

I was so sure
but now I see the truth.
Nobody is perfect
and neither are you.

All the sacrifices
you had to make.
All of your black stains
transformed into an impenetrable vein.

All of the voices
inside of my head,
shall remain distant,
away from my bed.

I know the truth.
My veins will always pump
this illuminating light
'till my heart stops to thump.

I was so su—

This is a new me!
This is who I am meant to be.
All of the questions I invested
shall now all be laid to rest.

I know the truth,
I am sure.

This is a new me.
This is who I am meant to be.

I am *sure*.

Dear Reader,

At this checkpoint, I ask that you take a moment to reflect.

The next chapter isn't for the faint of heart.

Trust in yourself always and listen to your intuition.

Intro 3: Disclaimer

This chapter is about Sexual Assault and Domestic Violence. If you have been a victim, I'm sorry. I'm here with you. Let us venture through this next chapter together. If you need to stop at any given time, allow your mind that break.

There is a list of resource numbers on page 235 if you need extra support. If you need someone to talk to, do not hesitate to reach out.

Keep fighting.

Keep pushing.

They're not here.

They can't hurt you.

You're powerful.

You're majestic.

You're free.

You're the compass

to a new beginning.

Chapter III
Consultation: Blinded by Darkness

Painted White Roses

Lately I've been reading books about love.
Stories of affection and songs about captivation
to help me create one of my own recognition.

Those are references.
Pages of chronicles that can't relate to my narration.

The pages to our book is being written every day
and here I lay feeling this emotion that can't be explained.

A gut reaction that can only be shown
in the darkest and lightest of days.

*Pain*ted white roses
*pain*ted red.

I promised you one day that I'd be able to write about love.
One that has the emotion of a thousand suns.

I, Gabriel, love thee with all of my being.
I will write and I will sing with all intensity and extremes.

You came to me cursed, and you picked up my broken shards.
Together, we melted our hearts and the rest we glued.

Love, not fear, aches for control.
I took you as you were.
My love, not a clone.
Not *fake* nor monotone.

There may be a limit.
There may be an end.
But for now
        "Till death do us part."
We'll tell our children.

*Pain*ted white roses
*pain*ted red.
*Pain*ted white roses.

The Greatest Force brought you to me
but it was our job to guide each other
in the right direction of history.

You see, everything happens for a reason,
if you had blundered down the wrong path
you would have stumbled across an apple
or needle to send you into a deep sleep.

That's how I was: asleep.

You see, I was trapped in an abyss
of nothingness and self-defeat.
The air was cold and
blisters scarred my feet.

The nightmare wouldn't end.
Then you came along with questions of the Zodiac
asking riddles only I could know.
It was that discussion that inspired us to grow.

*Pain*ted white roses
*pain*ted red.
*Pain*ted white roses
*pain*ted red.

So now after a short period of time here we are.

The fears and haunted memories
of my past are no more.
I've banished them to a time in place
only spoken in folklore.

Yes, at times we feel uneasy.
You should know, you don't have to please me
for I have loved you more than myself.
I assure you I will love no one else.

My heart was made out of ice,
and you set me free.

I Didn't Know... Love?

I didn't know Love could be
like this...
How is it possible for two people
to be so **close?**

    So *connected...*

I didn't know I could be loved
so deeply and so completely
for who I was and for who I wasn't.

In depthful ways, for
the first time I have truly felt
known.

I didn't know Love could
be so warming: the laughter, the joy,
or magical night adventures.

You ta-ta-take care of me.
Make me feel *safe* and protected.
      No matter what.

I L-love our growth and adaptability
as friends, lovers, and partners in life.

I *realize* now,
I still don't know Love,
because it was never
      you...

He Died

When I'm sad I'm a trickster.
When I'm mad I'm a threat.
I'm not bipolar but I do change my mood.
People often think I'm being rude.

If I cry until I fall asleep, what will you do?

> Will I come home
> to an empty chair,
> or smile because I know
> you're there?

If an argument becomes a fight, what will you do?

> Pack your bags and leave as
> I plead for you to stay,
> or close the door in silence
> 'till our anger sits at bay?

When I drive you insane
even though you know I'm playing a game,
will you shout with your lungs
or calmly speak my name?

When you ask about my past,
I fear you will leave.
There are no secrets, there are no lies,
yet you find an excuse to doubt and defy.

Someone died and I'm sad.
I'm playing a game,
trying to find reasons to be glad,
yet I'm driving you insane.

Black Rain

When I met you, you were
a person scarred by the darkest of darkness.

Black rain falls down, tainting our beings,
showering us with every ounce of inability
to sustain the truth of ever existing.

Except I want to know the truth.
I want to know the very fabric
that keeps you from getting
closer to me.

Repeating "I'm not good enough"
isn't going to push me away.

Just because you're internally damaged
doesn't mean you're damaged goods.

You're human and it's okay,
but please stop trying to push me away.

Black rain.
        Black rain.
                Black rain.

I crave to know what keeps you
        from crossing the line.

The line that you think will destroy me.
Except, if I may be honest,
you can't destroy dust.

In this life I experienced something
I only saw or heard on tv.

Something I never thought
would happen to me,
            yet it did.

I'm damaged and it hurts
because I'm afraid of getting *closer*.

In the end of what I thought was love
            was obsession.
What I saw in his eyes
            was a monster.

In yours, I see a caged soul.
One who doesn't think he's worthy.
One who so desperately
            wants to be rescued from—

Black rain.
            Black rain.
                        Black rain.

To end this narration.

You've seen darkness, a darkness so mad,
but within those dark, lost eyes I also see beauty.
Let go of what is and let in the light.
Cross the line and say goodbye to the poison.

Fight the darkness
because by rescuing you,
you set me free.

Black rain,
set me free.
            Black rain,
                        you've tainted me.

Black rain,
set me free.
　　　Black rain,
　　　you've awakened me.

Latrodectism

He was a beast
and I was his beauty
He was tangled in darkness
like a symbiotic creature.

A creature set out
thinking harm was acceptable.
A menace who preyed
on my old soul.

He was a black widow
and I was a fly
caught in his
web of lies.

His poison stung my heart.
His venom burned
as it made its way
through my *trusting* veins.

He weaved his way
throughout my life.

Gained the trust of those close to me.
Played it very carefully.
Even outsmarted me.

Listen to my tale,
listen to it very well.

He was one of a kind.
He disrespected and had no regards
to what I kept behind.

He had no self-control.
Pain was all he knew.

So sadistic,
   so masochistic.

The Garden of *Pain*ted White Roses
is where my body rests
covered in his vicious bites.

Infecting me with a fever.
A fever that was so wrong,
but felt so right.

Gripping on so ever tight,
his eyes watched me ever so closely.

Black Widow fever!

Your poison paralyzed
   my soul.

800-656-4673 (HOPE)

I hear your voice screaming at me
finding someone to blame for your insecurities.
I, a fresh breath of pure magic
can't find your shit to be tragic.

It's hilarious.

Your life's a drama, a joke.
Only time you were serious
was when your hands were
wrapped around my throat.

Your eyes dilated with a crimson rage
and forced me to beg for mercy
from your childish rampage.

I was waiting for you to change and rise
but you kept reveling in anger and pain.
It wasn't a surprise because the sadist
in your eyes always inflicted lies.

I was "with stupid" and
had confidence you'd change.
That was MY mistake.

My soul still hurts
and ALL I want, is to escape
        from your *grasp.*

*Pain*ted Black Roses

Lately I've been reading books about assault,
articles about survivors,
to help me create one of my own recognition.

But those are references.
Pages of chronicles that I can't relate to.

Navigating, though confused.
Confused of why he did what he did
like a child in an hourglass.

*Pain*ted white roses
*pain*ted black.

I promised myself I'd never let anyone
      hurt me again.
But here I am and my soul is
        scattered across space.

He was a cursed beast,
feeding off my dim light like a feast.
Like an old weak mirror, I finally shattered.
His *love* struck me again
                and again,
          and again.

I ache for peace.
      I ache for control.

His obsession
and insidious possession
split us apart.

*Pain*ted white roses
*pain*ted black.
*Pain*ted white roses.

Everything happens for a reason,
yet I'm at a loss for words as to
why he thought *this* was okay.

Once again I am trapped, and
riddled in nightmares and lost hope.

*Pain*ted white roses
*pain*ted black.
*Pain*ted white roses
*pain*ted black.

So now, after a short period
of time, here I am.
The fears and memories plague
          my mind.
The air I breathe is dead.

A sculpture of ice resembling
my heart rests
in the once blood-red cavity
of my chest.

Glass Heart

We could've done it all.
All I needed was your trust.

I had loved you
and you lost me.

This pain hurts like hell.

You tore my heart.
You split my mind.
How can I love again
if I can't even recognize myself?

You put your hands on my body
and made me feel so very special.
You told me you loved me,
yet when you placed your hands
            on me I fell.

My bruised body hurts like hell.

My heart has turned into glass.
My lungs burn to breathe.
I'm sitting in class pulling at my sleeves
because reminders are set underneath.

You told me you loved me
multiple times
as if it would make the trauma
            disappear.

Love isn't blind to the truth.
Love isn't placing your hands on me.
Love isn't forcing me down to have sex.

Love isn't a question you ask.
Love isn't jealousy.
Love isn't one-sided.
Love isn't anger.
Love isn't a war for control.
Love isn't inflicting pain for peace.
Love isn't how you loved me.

Piece by piece is how I told you
we'd help each other find peace.
But now piece by piece is all I am.

This pain hurts like hell.

I'm walking forward and rising,
yet a part of me is lost feeling
weak and ashamed.

The reflection I see before me
is a mystery
because the question I have is,

Where do I go from here?
        Who am *I* now?

Alone Again

He burned me with an intense fire
but I let the mistrust of my ex follow.

I miss the flame.

It's like a cold winter's breeze,
and I'm staring up at the lone bright stars
wondering if I'll ever get caught again?

There was this new guy I met
and I fucked up.

I can still feel him inside
holding on for dear life,
but the grand question is,
does he still want me at his side?

My heart was out of control.

Has my misfortune led us astray?

Here I lie alone again,
wishing you were here;
but I know the time that's past
can't be replaced.

Is this what I want my life to be?
Alone and by myself in misery?

I think I was falling for you,
but then I fell out of place.

You cared in a way
I thought no one would ever.

I weakened at your touch.
        I miss the feeling.

The words I write are more than just ink.
Lying in your arms makes the nightmares sink.
Because when I'm alone
I hear my ex's voice.

Here I lie alone again
wishing you were here,
but I know the time that's past
can't be replaced.

Is this what I want my life to be?
Alone and by myself in misery?

Ignoring all troubled signs
my eyes once saw
because life without you
makes me feel powerless and raw.

I've never felt so vulnerable.

Alone and in misery
is not what I want my life to be.

> *"So what if you have some darkness?*
> *Let's combine ours and make some light.*
> *You shouldn't be used. I care about you."*

        Do you still?

Here I lie alone again
wishing you were here,
but I know the time that's past
cannot be replaced.

Is this what I want my life to be?
Alone and by myself in misery?

This is not what I want
      my life to be...

Out of Order // Ghost

I try to not let myself be vulnerable.
        To show weakness.
        To let my guard down.

I trust people and my faith in others
        to do the right thing.

I tried to kill the pain,
but it only brought back more.

Nobody knows what goes on
        inside of my head.
Not even the poison that spreads.

I wear a mask surrounded by
        happiness,
            smiles,
                and laughter.

I've let go of my past
but starting over is so much
        harder.

I'm surviving on a blank white sheet of ice,
driving my soul to an unknown place
I hope to call home.

I am lost in a forest of souls.
        Seen but not visible.
        Heard but silenced.

I am light, and I am hope,
but most of all out of order
like a ghost in a broken machine.

Loose wired and rusty
left untouched,
        left unnoticed.

Seen only for what men desire;
        (a nice thick ass)
        but not for who I am.

I am d ri fti n g.

                loating.
        I am f

                I am a ghos

War[1]

It feels like I left home,
came back to a house
engulfed in flames
and no one will let me in.

What good am I if I can't help save
those who cared for me
when I was lying in my grave?

What good am I if I can't be
the person they need me to be,
someone who's brave?

For years I was a slave
in my own head.
Depression caught me
like a spinning thread.

It had weaved itself from
my mind and into my soul,
repressing the love and leaving
nothing but an empty hole.

Since I was an empty shell
with this strange beating sound
I left my roots to find a new tune,
but had found myself trapped in hell

created by my own malevolent spell.
The outside world seemed like a mirage.
Everything was out of place,
even those who called my name.

---

1 Content warning: mention of self-harm.

To keep myself hidden from more pain
I camouflaged my heart. It matched my soul,
so the darkness devoured the last beating light.
Now they were the same.

Tears escaped my bloodthirsty wrists.
It had been years since I last cut
but cutting only brought more rumor-feeding eyes,
and so the razor never fed.

It came inches from my starving skin,
but I had to desist.

Suicide will not be how I die.

Through years of both
mental and emotional pain
coexisting but never the same.

I found my voice and became very wise.
I learned how to save a life in this twisted game
we call life. To my surprise

I was the voice they needed me to be
not someone who I thought I needed to be.

Here I am now still fighting the soldiers
who came from the portal
of lost hope and empty dreams.

Through the blood, sweat, and tears
I finally have light and it's magical.

Fight until your last breath.
Fight until fight is just a word.
Fight until the hole is sealed.
Fight until you can smile.

Fight until you feel joy.
Fight until you find your voice.
Fight and say no.
Fight for the dream.
Fight and reclaim what was yours.
Fight until you break the front door to your home.
Fight until the flames are extinguished.
Fight and rise.

PTSD[2]

It's been one year since you choked me down
gasping for a fresh breath of life.
You were the predator and I had become
   Your prey.

The anger in your eyes
told me I wasn't going to see
the next day.

When I was able to speak
I demanded you to stop.

I smacked your arm.
I cursed your name,
but the possession
   you were under
crippled me in chains.

With a stroke of your hand
you pulled down my shorts.
With another went down yours.

Before the room became stars
and the sound of my breathing
became but a single beeping tone,

I heard you spit.
First word that came to mind was shit.
Out of all the words in the dictionary
I said shit.

---

2 Content warning: sexual violence.

Your eyes were as demonic as
your finger penetrating deep inside.
I could taste the nail clawing
as if it were alive.

I heard you spit once more.
I was trying so hard to clench my anus
but your hunger for pain withdrew me.

I felt the tip.

Tears broke out.

This was it.
I knew this was it.

It's been one year and the haunted
memories pick at my brain
            like a parasite
leaving me wide awake and
            ashamed.

My soul is obliterated;
            smashed into pieces.

You motherfucker,
            you murdered my soul!

For fucks sake leave me the hell alone!

I'm like a zombie.
Deprived from sleep
and when I do sleep
all I hear are the sounds of my cries,
            the sounds of my screams.

Because you terrorize
        the only place I can escape to!

I wake up screaming!
Tugging at my throat
because I've forgotten
how to breathe!

My friends ask,
        "What's wrong Gabey?"

                "Nothing.
                        I'm fine.
                                Just tired."

It's been one year and yet
I'm still dancing with
        your ghost.

Become

I was born ready to live,
but not ready to survive
the countless challenges
I had to face and overcome:

> Bullying
> Suicide
> Coming Out
> Assault
> Threats of Violence
> Near Death Experiences
> Health Issues
> Molestation
> Rape
> Abuse

All things that are a part
of life and it's fucked up.

Each one carries a significant
lesson.

Learning the lesson,
>   growing,
>   and getting stronger
>   *for the next one.*

No one knows your story
unless you share it.

I survived suicide
not because of people
stopping me.

I survived because
I realized there was so much
more to life, but I also knew
there would be so much more *pain*.

So, I changed my story
and now I help change others too,
even if they don't want me to.

That shadow in the corner,
the whisper in your ear,
I will be there as much as I can.

leaving breadcrumbs of my light
to brighten up the darkness in you.

I know what it's like
to live in an influential world
of complete darkness.

The feeling of blood
running down your arm.
            To feel the world against you.
            People pushing you against walls.
            Going home with bruises and scars.

I get it.

Being terrorized because you're different.

Own the difference.
Own your originality
because the moment you give
others a chance, they'll win.

Never be afraid to make a difference.
Lead by example and rise.

So, fight and change your story.

Creation

When the world seems dark, we run and hide.
We shut everything and everyone out.
When we do this we're letting the darkness in,
a vicious monster of absolute chaos.

Stare outside your open window.

Hear and feel everyone's emotions.

Shut the window and tune it all out.

If you close the blinds your vision obscures.
The voices subside.
The light is on in your room.
The light is your friend,
but you turn it off.
Darkness.
You've been enveloped in darkness.
Alone and weak.
Tired of all the lies.
Hating everyone including yourself.
Angry at the world.
Sad and broken; defeated.

"You have to want to be helped."

Find the courage to turn on the light.
Rip open the blinds.
Shatter the window.
Let all the emotions in.
Hear the innocents.
Be your own hero.
Become a Guardian.

And let the world know
exactly who

the

hell

You

are.

Complete Without You

I feel so lost, yet so complete.
Love he was, but love I'm not.
I'm no longer fighting the sheets:
the hallucinating hell I once lived.

I'm rising from the ashes
he had left me in.

Every now and then I get a flash
of how I was then:

      Weak.
              Confused.
         Tortured.
              Broken.

He's not here, yet the scars are.
        It's finally time **I let you go**.

Wherever you are,
wherever you may be,
I forgive you.
Not for you, but for me.

Fighting the past.
Pushing through the madness.
I'm living for me and unfazed
by your vicious ways.

Rebuilding myself piece by piece
has never been a rapturous release.

You're not here, nor are the scars.
        I've let you go.

I'm no longer confused
of the life I choose.
Beginning anew
without you.

I'm rising from the ashes
you left me in.
Fighting the abusive past.
Pushing through the madness.
Unfazed by your vicious ways.

I'm not hallucinating the hell
I once lived.
Not fighting the sadistic sheets.

I feel lost—
correction, *felt*—
and now I feel complete.

Pledge of Guardianship

I pledge allegiance
to the lost and forgotten.

I align myself with those around me
      to guard and to protect,
      to help and to serve,
      to care for and take responsibility

of the innocents
I have sworn to protect
whenever and wherever I am.

As long as I live.

Blessed be.

Hello Beautiful,

At this *Checkpoint* I ask you to step away if you need to. This chapter was difficult to write, and I can only imagine what you're thinking and if you had any triggers. If you've made it this far, thank you. Thank you for fighting with me.

Acknowledge your triggers.
Acknowledge who you are.
Acknowledge your growth.

You are safe.

Now let us take a deep breath together:

Inhale, 2, 3, 4.
Exhale, 2, 3, 4.
Inhale, 2, 3, 4.
Exhale, 2, 3, 4.
Last one.
Inhale, 2, 3, 4.
Exhale, 2, 3, 4.

Appreciate and honor yourself always.

Chapter IV
*Die*agnosis: Faces of Evil

Intro 4

The traumatic experience left a malevolent door open leading to Pandora's Box.

Diagnosed with Post Traumatic Stress Disorder, unraveled the depths of the human mind.

The next chapter of rhymes and abstract poetic art is not distinct to any or one physical form.

Let your mind be free of noise to counter disturbing and wicked trauma.

Lucid

When you lie awake at night shaken
from a dream without words,
do you still hear the voices?

Do you still hear them tantalize your thoughts?

Can you still see their empty faces
glaring from the shadows and hollowed spaces?

When you lie awake in the dead, whisper, night,
how do you know if you're truly awake?

CODE RED

CODE RED!

ATTENTION, CODE RED!

The fire pierced my eyes.
Tried to figure out if it was real
or just a hallucinogenic trick.

Adrenaline grabbed a fire extinguisher.
Next thing you know I'm aiming at the
conjured wicked beast.

For a second, it died, but then
it burst like it was angry and alive.
Fighting back, it felt like my body burned.
The flames scorched my skin, and the smoke…
the sinister smoke burned my soul.

My gaze was fixated on the fire.
The blazing flames paralyzed my limbs.
Inhaling, I choked; gasping,
searching for a fresh breath of air.

I was lost in the smoke:
        trapped.

My path to escape was gone.

The smoke had blinded my sight.

> *"Can anyone hear me?"*
> *"I can't find my way out!"*
> *"Somebody help me!"*

I heard the sound of screams
throughout every direction.
Then the blistering sound
of the Fire Alarm captivated
        my soul.

The hypnotic sound
took hold of
        my mind.

I am lost...

I am lost...
        In the smoke.

CODE RED!

ATTENTION, CODE RED!

PLEASE MAKE YOUR WAY
TO THE NEAREST EXIT!

CODE RED!

Revenant

The appendages added to my limbs feel numb.
I wake to the persistent torment of my wrists
and ankles.
When dire, I wear braces and bands like some
sort of mummy, and it makes me feel less human.

It makes me feel sick and weak.
Last night I had a few drinks to numb the pain,
but alcoholism isn't an answer to chronic illness.
I hope to one day wake up and this discomforting
            torture will be nonexistent.

The joints connected to my limbs feel lost.
I wake to the determined harrowing where
muscles and bone meet.
When dire, I wear braces and bands like some sort of undead
creature, and it makes me feel unidentifiable.

It makes me feel revolting and frail.
It makes me feel like an alien to my own skin.
Last night I had a few blunts to numb the pain,
but I lost track of time.

Smoking the hybrid made me hallucinate a world
where I'd wake up from this discomforting
torturous hell. Where I was able to fully come alive without being
overwhelmed and constantly having a full-fledged war within
            my own body.

When I was snapped back to reality, I cried.
I cried hard because it was a life I'd never truly have. A life I'd only
be able to feel with my fingertips before being pushed back into
purgatory

            for the crime
                    of wanting to live.

Vengeance: There Must Be a Reason

There must be a reason.
There must be….
There must be a *reason*.

There must be a reason why
I can never have a break.
Does it happen before or after
my heart's strings sever and ache?

I'm trying so fucking hard
not to be enraged.

Lord have mercy.

The negative and active emotions
building up inside fuels the outrage
like a volcanic eruption
ready to activate its rampage.

My soul was murdered
some time ago, yet the people
around me seem to think I am
       "*Okay*."

I'm not.

People who barely know me
know me better than those who I call
family.

It's really hard to keep
them close to me
when the world I know
is falling apart.

I feel like I'm hallucinating.
Trying to make sense of what is real.
What's real feels like a mistake.
Father, God, please help me heal.

Close ties became white lies
when her boyfriend took offense.

Great. So, let me get this straight.
You're the birth of my blood,
yet you're choosing one side.
I thought it would've been mine!

He flicked your heart like
turning the lights on in a haunted house.

After you said you'd stand by my side,
you chose to fight for him.
Figures, you always tossed me aside.

Your love is toxic and manipulative
and I am gullible for falling for it
every time because you're my
                mother.

You're the reason why
it's so hard for me to find
Love;
the moment I have it,
I don't trust it.

I called you out,
and you said it yourself,
you pay more attention to
one kid than the other.

Well guess what?

Now, you don't have to.

You've pushed me so hard
I don't want any part of it.
You've pushed me so hard
out the door that I've locked
    myself out.

I see you spread your love,
but for me, all I get are the
    leftovers…

I feel like I'm hallucinating.
Trying to make sense of what's real.
Everything feels like a mistake.
My soul has been trying to heal.

Jesus fucking Christ!

I am the anger of the monsters
in the wall.

I feel like I woke up in a nightmare.

I can't… I don't…
understand.

Do you even care?
Is this what love does to us?

Stand by your husband
and leave the child to
survive?

I'm spiraling down a path
filled with resentment and hate.

I believe it's best I pack up
all of my shit and leave for the last
time.

I don't think you'll miss much.

I feel like I'm hallucinating.
Trying to make sense of what is real.
What's reality feels like a mistake.
My soul can't heal.

The vengeance is maddening.
It's reactivating the void in my chest.
The wicked dark thoughts of
haunted ghosts and false perceptions.

The light is slipping away,
and I'm praying for it to come back.
On my knees, the cold cracked cement
feels just like my cold dying heart.

I don't know how I will survive this time.

There must be a reason.
        There must be…
There must be a reason.
        There must be…

        a reason.

Sovereignty's Fury

I feel the fury closing in.
I have no sense of when or where to begin.
I feel the madness in my soul.
The only feeling I feel is the blistering cold.
It's a mad thought to feel left out.
      Left out of the conversation.
      Left out of the gatherings.
      Left out of my own body.
My body has been in a 20-year war.
Depression isn't a joke. It's real, and it will
petrify every living,
              breathing,
                     and idiosyncratic form
about you.
Which is why sovereignty over the mind is
so fucking important.
It's like an undertaking of
your own emotional existence
tearing at you like a savage
shadow of your own creation.
It monitors when you breathe
and when you're able to scream
      for help.
But when you do scream for help,
it plays a trick on your friends
telling them, "I'm okay."
Those are the voices in my head,
not the friendly, happy voice you know.
It's a corrupt, tall-tale response
told by the infamous vicious monster
      inside.
A white precious lie underneath the
defective,

pulverized,
cracked skin.
I wish life was like an Etch-A-Sketch
because then I could draw the
depression and then shake it up and
start over with a fresh canvas.
My tears cry for salvation.
I weep,
and I weep,
and I weep,
but the tears are but a fragment
of the profusive illusions
dancing in my head.
Lord, I surrender any piece of soul
I have left.
I dream of the day, the fury inside
will eventually but surely subside
because this madness has stricken
the light and I am terrified.
I feel the fury beginning to rise.
The vultures are here to collect my soul.
They're circling the fragments left out.
If swallowed, then the last beating light
will vanish into nothingness, and I will be
nothing.
But that's just it.
I am something.
I am **someone**.
I will not fall to the wings of death.
I will not become ash above a fireplace.
This fury will be the embodiment
of my resurrection because as I sit
here looking at the time that's passed,
reminiscing of the darkness that
stalked me home,
crept inside,
and assaulted me,

will not overtake;
will not triumph;
will not corrupt any longer;
I will become the north star
and guide myself **home**.

Blinded by Smoke

The darkness creeps and screams my name.
It warps my soul like the withdrawal of an addiction.
Sixteen years ago it set a virus into my mainframe.
Now, without notice, it plans to attempt a final eviction.

Screaming at the words on the billboards.
The tantalizing advertisement smiles
like it knows my pain.
Like it knows the truth I can't say:
the truth of a dying soul.

The truth is, I am so unbelievably lost.
It feels like I have no one.
It feels like no one understands, as if my words
are getting lost in translation.

I can't see!
        I can't feel!
I can't breathe!

RAH!

I'm fucking numb to the "inspirational" quotes.

I have no passion.
I have no drive.

I'm not living because the trauma cornered me.
It forced me to push everyone away.

My soul is slipping away and feels
like it can't hold on *any longer*.

I tried to be you and follow in your footsteps,
but you're stronger than I am. I want to be where
you are but for every step I take forward,
the shadows keep you five feet ahead.

      I am tired...
            of living...
                    this way...

Ne Me Cadere

Holding on to feel loved.
Holding on until I can't anymore.

Emotionally I've never felt so alone.
It's like the quiet dead space
meeting the silence of my ringtone.

My person distracts me with books and music,
but sometimes it isn't enough.

The darkness is sinking in condemning my soul.
Ejecting the remaining light from the shoal.
This silent predator has come again.
        It's hard to break away.

Fighting the possession like a child's tantrum.
This war is my anthem.

Maybe this is why I feel abandoned.

When the darkness plays my soul
like a harp, I can feel its razor-sharp
        claws around my heart.

It comes and goes in ways,
in ways I can't even begin to explain.

Sometimes I feel like no one wants me.
"Do you even think about me?"
        —I wonder.

I call out to the heavens
until my throat is dry and sore.
I call out because all I want
is to be close to the shore.

To be close to human skin.
The closeness of another body
and linking our minds
in wondrous conversational binds.

I get the closeness
of the cold wooden floor.
No one comes knocking at my door.
Fuck, this has to be a brand-new score!

Ugh!

Sadness is all I know.
It tiptoes back and forth between
the curtain like a ravaging sideshow.

They watch and they stare.
I don't want an audience
I don't want pity, I just want
someone to care.

Fuck!

I'm so mad that I feel this way.
My soul wants to restore
but the anger is like a spore
searching for ignition in a drugstore.

First, men say they adore me.
They say they want to meet me.
Then the encore of a used line,

> *"I'm sorry but I'm going through a lot right now."*

Like fuck, I am too!

But why did you mentor
my heart to jump and to explore

the possibility if you were just going
to open a trapped door?

Loneliness is hard to rest
when you can't breathe.
Floating towards the sky
like the empty thoughts you couldn't apply.

I'm dragging my body
across the cold, wet sand
because I have to…

I have to keep going.
I have to hold on.

Not for love, but for myself
because this story in a book
wants off this fucking bookshelf.

I'm holding on.
I'm holding on. (Don't let me fall)

There's a mad, twisted, darkness inside,

but as long as I don't give in,
         I'll be fine.

I need to rise higher than before.

                 I need to accept the darkness.

                         I need to have faith and belief.

                 The light may burn, but it's better than this,
                                 so I will strive to rise.

Wicked Current

In this body,
        I am lost.
Moving slowly and moving fast.
There was a bridge
and on this bridge, I found myself
fighting for life.
I stared at the asphalt ground
wanting to dive, and plunge.
Plunge into the darkness and forget.
Forget about the pain, guilt, and all
        I had regret.
But there was a woman
with eyes white as lilies.
She asked if I was okay?
Tears burned my face because
the thought of death was at my
        fingertips.
Her question,
        her concern,
                she said it would
    get **better**.
 With raging voices and feelings
        of eternal darkness,
I walked away from the bridge.
        I walked,
                and walked,
                        and walked
until I smelled the ocean.
Plopping myself onto the cold sand,
it had been a cloudy day,
I stared at the crashing waves
and had a wicked thought.
        What if I walked into the water?

What if I set myself adrift?
What if I let the current take me prisoner?
Oh, what if?
Thinking these thoughts,
I cried once more.
Staggering to fulfill the action
but when the moment came,
I stopped.
I received a phone call.
It was from my mother.
It was as if she knew.
Maybe God told her to?
I fought back the tears and worry
in my throat.
She asked me what was wrong, but I lied.
She asked me what time I'd be home.
To my response,
"I don't know?"
What is a home without happiness?
What is love without loving yourself?
What is everything if you feel nothing?
What is life if you're constantly battling Death?
Ah!
Life can truly be wicked
but we mustn't forget.
No matter which current
you're moving in, it isn't forever.
You have the power to keep going,
and swim to tomorrow.
I know tomorrow sounds like a myth.
Some of us won't think it exists
It does.
Then a week turns into a month,
and then a month turns into a year,
and so forth.
Keep fighting and find a reason to **live**.

Get lost,
                lose money,
        get drunk,
                get high,
        get a bad grade,
                and fail!
Failing is the best teacher.
It shows us the person in the mirror.
I am incredibly lost right now,
but I no longer want to die.
I want to love, experience, and live.
I want to meet the person in the mirror
                in ten years.
Life can be wicked.
It's okay to be lost
because then we can
                find our soul
in what we truly love.
This riptide, this current,
can't devour you if you fight
hard enough and swim away.
Like my friend Dory says,
        "Just keep swimming.
                Just keep swimming."
Just keep,
        keep,
                keep...

Black Ice

Ice falls on this black road.
I've been on it for far too long.
It's so dangerous when you
can't see the snow.

Here you are standing in front of me
acting as though what you did wasn't
        purposefully.

You wonder why my heart was so cold.
You asked me how the color of my eyes
changed from brown to black to gold?

It was society's influence.

My identity was assumed.
Before I could speak, the world
exposed my privacy and then
they saw me as weak.

They threw rocks and swung
their fists. Never had I felt so alone.
I looked up at the twinkling sky
and shouted HIS name.

That night, I lost faith
in all humanity and shut down.

Since people were so hateful,
I wore a disguise.
I couldn't voice my opinion,
and so I spat lies.

Every day I felt this fury of ice
building deep inside.

I deprived myself of feeling
love or happiness.

I was so cold.

As time moved forward
I broke the armor of glass.

You meant what you did.
It was no accident.

I may have changed who I was
but never will it change
who I am.

Society's influence brought out
the darkness inside but never will it
regain control over my soul.

Ice may fall on your road
but know you're never alone.

Life can be dangerous,
especially if you can't see
the snow.

Bedbug

Do you not realize the parasitic vampire you are?

A devastation to my bloodline.

You watch and you stare, but you don't do anything.

You're so hazardous, like Chernobyl's nuclear air.

      Withering roses, ashes to ashes.

Open your eyes and realize the damage you're causing.

Truly awaken to the sickness because the harbinger is calling.

Symphony of Devastation

We live.
We suck.
We love.
We fuck.

We sing.
We dance.
We praise
romance.

A love I search for
buried deep within the snow.
I hear your soul whisper
within the cries of a crow.

We climb.
We run.
We fight.
Getting high in the sun.

We drink.
We joke.
We never saw tomorrow;
you overdosed on a line of coke.

A love so deep
I en*vision*-ed.
I'm curious, I wonder,
as I stare at the broken flowers
        I used to destroy;
        the dandelions are gone
                and so are you.

I watched years pass.
I grew and aged.
  Without you,
    I turned the page.

Onward
  to a brand
    new
      life.

I cried.
I yelled.
I b r o k e
  into a sweet
    symphony of devastation.

You weren't there
  but truthfully,
  you never
  were.

A few dozen roses
lay on your tombstone,
  YET
     Not a single soul knows
     the hexed horror of poses
     I endured to satisfy
     your vexed sinister clone.
As I dance on your grave
drinking a bottle of tequila,
I am not sad that you died
but I'm also not satisfied
that you aren't alive.
  The venom you injected
  continues its attempt to override
  and I'm in disbelief that the years

that have passed, you're *still*
      a threat to my mind.

Maybe if I didn't have a soul
it would be easier to smoke
    this bowl.
I've become a starving alcoholic!
The tides have turned
    and I feel
        Alive.

~~Grateful~~

I should be grateful to be alive
       right?
To breathe, to walk, to move around
       on my own.
I *should* be grateful.

However, I feel palpitations
across my abdomen.
They're terribly painful.
It's a sudden sharp pain.

"Are you stressed?"
       I was sleeping peacefully.

The doctors ask the same question
as if the history across my arms
manifested the symptoms to
the mysterious condition.

Urgent Care, labs, appointments,
Check-ups, follow ups.
Money down the drain,
a cabinet of prescribed drugs.

Yet no diagnosis.

No conclusion to the reason
I can't sleep. No reason for blood
to launch from my bowels.
Labs are inconclusive,
but I'm still alive.

Shaking.
Breathing.
Tolerating a threat
to my well-being.

So, who the absolute fuck are you
to tell me I should be grateful?

NAFLD (Non-Alcoholic Fatty Liver Disease)

Your beautiful red skin
is soft like tissue.
Your body is triangular
yet also round.

You're very popular in a crowd
for you have many functions.

At the party,
you're detoxifying chemicals
and processing drugs.

You love to filter supplies
as they come.
However, you also
      Digest,
      Absorb, and
      Metabolize
them too.

If the party begins to hemorrhage,
you stabilize the clot of humans.
You never seem to fail.
You somehow save the day.

But if you get passed around
you begin to die
a slow, painful death.

You filtered the wrong
things.
But you didn't know
any better.

You were just doing your job
without question or hesitation.
Now, your life's on the line,
and I'm trying to save you.

I'm trying so hard
to rewrite your mutation.
To deflate your addictive
and intoxicating behavior.

You used to taste
so marvelously delicious.
Now as I bite into
your soft crimson flesh,

You...

       Taste...

             Like...

                   Death...

Hallucinations: It Lurks from Within

Tsk, tsk.
I watch you when you sleep.
Tossing and turning as you weep.

Tsk, tsk.
Blood draws from razor sharp claws.
The shadow lurks, acidic drool running down their jaws.

Tsk, tsk.
Can't you see them in the crooked halls?
They're crawling on the crisp scorched walls.

Tsk, tsk.
Sweating, my head draws back.
My body contorts, my spine splinters: crack!

Tsk, tsk.
Wide awake yet paralyzed;
a sweet slumbering demise.

When *He* Lurks Near

My skin presents, *"I'm fine,"*
but my body twists and cracks.
"I'm okay," is an overused line.
I taste the smoke of the cannabis
that burns on the opposite end
of the hybrid packed bowl.
My soul drifts trying to ascend,
yet my ribcage can't expand like it *used to.*

The candle flame dances so bright.
I want to touch the powerful flames,
but my energy is weakened by the blight
growing through the silhouette

between my organs and tissue.
I died, and for a minute, I was relieved.
The pain seized, but then I spewed
blood… My body hunched forward,

belched, and tightened until my throat
stung, and then the room turned black.
The fear I had feared for months was afloat
in my crimson-stained toilet bowl.

He, the Angel of *Death* howls like a banshee.
Lurking in the shadows like a hungry wolf,
he taunts me with damnation as I pray for mercy.
He glares with a crooked smile as I choke for air.

Every day I feel weaker to the transgression
of my mutated, waning cells.
I'm so sad yet filled with so much aggression
because now that I want to live,
   I am dying.

The Cure

If I were going to die today,
what would you tell me?
What would you say?

The final words
are always worth
more than gold.

The things we say
the things we do
in the end
is what matters most.

To relieve yourself
of the wicked thoughts
perched in your mind.

To feel the comfort
of being forgiven
or the madness from not.

You don't want to wake up one day
            with regret.

If I died
and you said nothing
how would you feel?

The ability to speak and hear
those last words
are a blessing or a curse.

The ability to feel and see them
one last time before their passing
is a gift, is a cure.

So if you knew
I was going to die today,
what would you tell me?
What would you say?

If **you** *knew*
I was going to die today,
what would you tell me?
What would you say?

Mercy

It's so cold outside
　　　It's so cold.
It's so cold outside.
　　　It's so cold.

Every day is a war
to take control of my body,
my limbs. It feels
as if they aren't mine.

My body hurts to rise
and shine. It aches
for a remedy. I'm so tired
of fighting.

I cry
and I cry
　　　for mercy.

My body talks
with such violence.
My chest burns to breathe
crushing as it expands.

Within this body, lies
answers doctors can't find.

What good is my money
if they can't find a cure?
They fill my body with pills
just as quickly as my wallet
　　　empties.

Yet here I am,
        still in pain.

It's so cold outside.
        It's so cold.
It's so cold outside.
        It's so cold.

Life can be so cruel.
When you finally think
you're on top,
lightning strikes.

For a moment,
I was at peace.
I felt indestructible,
I felt relinquished.

Then I woke up.
This is my reality
and it sucks.

Memories I have, have faded
leaving my brain hollowed
and fidgeting to remember
what's already lost.

Curling up into a ball
praying the agony away,
asking him to please
set me free.

> *"I don't want to die*
> *but I'm so tired of fighting*
> *Lord."*

I cry
and I cry
      for mercy.

It's so cold outside.
      It's so cold.
and I'm crying for
      MERCY.

Wil-O'-the-Wisp

When we sleep,
        where do you think
                our minds travel?
Do we venture off into another realm?
        Do we teleport our spirits
                or project our conscience?
Because sometimes,
        I wake with dirty hands.
        I wake to a deep pain in my chest.
        I wake to blood drying on my lips.
        I wake to bruises scattered on my arms.
        I wake to lesions down my back.

So, when do we sleep?
        Are we ever awake?
                or maybe
                        we already
                                are…

Obliviate

Erase the ties that bind from a life before.
Untangle the souls and let them soar.
Obliviate their faces and leave no trace.
Wipe their tracks and leave them efface.
When the clock strikes twelve
and then every hour a memory will vanish.
This is my will, this is my power.
By the Goddess of the Moon, set me free.
Eradicate my heart.
Blessed be.

Hello Dear Passenger,

I see you made it through another chapter.

I know that was a tough battle with reality, but we made it.

For every challenge that enters my path, every lesson in life, every tragedy, every negative and or everyday real life horror, I am still alive.

Chapter V
Treatment

Intro 5

Venture forth
as we transform ourselves
into another reality and truly begin
the process of
       healing.

It's Okay

It's okay to let go
and walk away
from the present.

It's okay to feel
the waves of
unknown emotion.

It's okay to feel
the rampaging guilt
of traumatic ghosts.

It's okay to scream
at the faceless
possibilities of death.

It's okay to feel,
because without emotions
we become inhuman.

Remember to Be Human

I want to remember what it was like to be human;

I want to remember what it was like to smile at nothing yet everything at the same time.

I want to remember what it was like to smell the frozen roses during a crisp winter's night.

I want to remember what it was like to see people be kind to each other without regression.

I want to remember what it was like to hear the words of peace and forgiveness without retaliation.

I want to remember what it was like to touch another living soul without fear.

I want to remember what it was like to connect to another heart without being broken and ghosted.

I want to remember what it was like to love, because the world we live in now is polluted by a thick cloud of hatred.

I want to remember what it was like to watch someone stand up against the disgusting hate.

I want to remember what it was like to be human, because being human now is like Halloween, pretending to be what you are in public and becoming who you are at home.

I want to remember what it was like to be human. Maybe I didn't even know at all...

Guardian Angel

It was a dark day.
The cold clouds had surrounded the bay.
I woke up in the shadows.
The only light had come from you.

Your red lips and stylish hair,
your ghostly skin, and chilling
voice gave me a scare.

It was the last time
I heard you speak.
It was the last time
I heard you breathe.

You told me everything
would be okay.
You told me not to worry
and you no longer felt pain.

I watched your spirit rise
to the sky and fade
as the greatest force
reached out and called
              your name.

It was the last time
I saw you smile.
It was the last time
I saw you there.
It was the last time.

The last time.

Our sweet angel,
your time had come.

From time and space,
you departed this place
returning to him,
the hands of grace.

> *"We set you free.*
> *We'll always share*
> *your memories.*
> > *We're watching over her*
> > *as she watched over you.*

> *We're all okay.*
> *We know you couldn't stay.*

It was the last time
I saw your smile.
It was the last time
I saw you there.
> It was the last time
> I heard your voice.
> It was the last time
> I heard your heart
> > beating.

> *"Wherever you are*
> > *I hope you're okay.*
> > *Always and forever*
> > > *in our hearts."*

I love you.
Blessed be,
> Desiree Ann Murry.

In Memory
November 20, 1989–December 12, 2010

Feel to Heal

Why does it matter?

I'm floating in a sea of death
trying to escape the vexed
horrors of reality.

Will it get better?
The round, hard, softball-sized
Magic 8-Ball, after being shook says,

> *"Try again later."*

A family I see through a square.
Their pixelated faces smile and stare.
A family that I wish and hope to see
but every time I hope,

> someone from my childhood
> dies.

I want to hope, wish, and pray
but as time goes by, the hope
begins to diminish by the
disturbed death of a generation.

> I...
> > Can't...

> Cry...

It feels stuck.

Truthfully, I don't want to feel it.
So, instead I've been feeding off
the pain of others.

The sadness in my throat
is at war
with the anger in my chest.

It's so easy to be numb.

It hurts so much to feel.

Feel the loss.
   Feel the death.
Feel the fire in your chest.
   Feel the agony in your throat.
Feel and let go.
   Feel and scream.

Feel, to begin the process
   to heal.

Scars and Labels

When I was a student
at Dodson Middle School,
I felt like I had been cursed.

Every day students were hostile.

Sixth grade, at Peck Park,
        I had been approached.
I had been attacked
        for being a word I didn't know then

Gay.

She stared into my eyes,
fixated on my soul,
and saw what I had not yet
known.

Her cold gaze will always linger
in my mind. My soul was crippled.
I couldn't breathe.

Seventh grade Algebra:
the crucial hauntings began.
Someone was playing
with my hoodie.

Pulling it away,
something had fallen.
Looked down and saw paper.

Odd.

This paper did not make sense.
Something about it lured
me to grab it, yet I didn't.

While walking down the path
to my next class, some kid
pushed me against the wall.

They walked away laughing.

I raised up my hoodie and there dangling
in front of my eyes were post-it notes.

"Punch Me"

"Kick Me"

"Push Me"

"Poke Me"

"I'm Gay"

"I'm Ugly"

"I'm Fat"

The list goes on…

My eyes would swell from the tears.
It lasted for a year.

The only place I felt safe
were the bathrooms or at home.
Never had I ever felt more alone.

They were insidious.

Creeping up on me.
These labels were a crooked image
of how they saw me.

I couldn't take the pain anymore

For the first time, blood spilled.

I would wear my sweater
even if it wasn't the weather
because I had to hide the weakness
I had to hide the [pain].

Thirty-eight:
the number of scars
I drew across my arms
when I was caught.

Doctors and therapists
were baffled on how a sweet kid
could self-harm.

I told them my story.

The next day,
the reason behind my pain,
the intruder who stole my name
wasn't in any of my classes.

He had been expelled.
However, the system
can't expel twenty other
students.

So, I pleaded with my mother
to transfer me to another school
where I had friends.

The transfer was done
but soon after came another disaster.

I was jumped once again,
but this time I was Gay.
This time my identity
was caught in a rumor.

People knew.
I couldn't lie nor hide.
Nowhere was safe.

> *"Two more weeks till graduation*
> *then it's high school,"*

I would tell myself.

We moved during the summer,
so I had the chance to start over.
A town who didn't know me.
A school with faces who were aliens to my mind.

I felt anxious and strange.
My body had morphed.
I was bullied, and so
I shut down.

After two years,
the people who knew me then
saw the person they knew was reborn.

I told my story and helped others
believe in themselves.
I was a vision for hope.

Forever will I have the scars
from years past but I will also
carry a label.

Accept yourself and live
because living in darkness
isn't the place for anyone.

Today,
I am proud to be a Gay Latino.

Beautiful Trauma

Sirens,
I hear them approaching
the scene of my demise.

Figures,
they exit their patriotic cars
with pale white faces.

Past,
is a cryptic white lie
folded into the closet.

Truth,
a shadow seduced
my *child*hood.

Forward,
I attempted to slice
the delicate skin on my wrists.

5150,
an obtuse, white and blue room,
and wide-eyed patrolling neighbors.

Community,
they wander the department
screaming and shouting.

I,
in an unknown state
of panic and fear.

Evaluation,
I *feel* to a great extent
and others see dramatics.

Diagnosis,
Hypersensitivity and
Major Depressive Disorder.

Treatment,
bi-weekly sessions with a paradoxical
Psychologist attempting to restore my soul.

Prognosis,
a search for my soul
through winding pine trails.

Acceptance,
by a well, I said goodbye
to the harbingers of my past.

Present,
I forgave the hungry revenants,
moved on, and filled my heart with
        joy.

Crossroads of Destiny

When I was a boy
I'd have dreams
of when I was a man.

The appearance of myself and
of strangers were familiar,
yet I never recognized
them until now.

Now that I'm all grown up,
those strangers I dreamt of
are dear close friends.

Like the band Green Day,
I used to walk a road alone.
It was empty, sad, and filled with
disappointment and doubt.

Through the years, the road
wasn't so lonely.
The road soon filled with acquaintances
who now I can call family.

Though the sadness I had
has faded, at times I feel empty,
but the difference from before,
now I know I'm not alone.

When the darkness wants me
to be alone, my anomalous family
rescues my soul and guides it home.

When a shadow speaks to me
in the mirror to split my skin,

my friends patrol my thoughts
cheering me on that I can win.

When my friends push my ability
to rise, I feel the weight on my shoulders
subside. They help carry my toxic,
weak extremities on to the next day.

Sometimes I wonder,

> *"Why do I deserve you?"*

Sometimes I wonder,

> *"Where would I be without you?"*

For the road I walk on is no longer empty.
The road I walk on will not prevent me
from my future dreams.

The road I walk on isn't lonely
anymore.
The road I walk on
fills my heart with so much more.

Joy I thought I'd never have,
yet here we are, and here I am.

I'm still fighting the plague
ensnared in my body like a virus
in a program.

You invaded my soul
with a blazing fire of light.
You assaulted my heart
with love, desire, and might.

You're my unspoken happiness
and kindling flame.
You're the bonus level
of a Super Mario game.

I know wherever I go,
I just have to close my eyes
and think of you.

For the boulevard I walk on
isn't one of broken dreams.
I know the road will never be empty
for I share it with those I call **family**.

Dollhouse

Under the stars
you were born.
The constellation of Gemini
gave me your eyes.

You have influenced and guided.
You have pushed and inspired.
Born of pain, you created love.
Endured the scut, you rose above.

Under the stars
you were born.
You took on a special role
and gave me a soul.

Surrounded by love,
you created a home.
You have never needed a spouse
to create a family or build a house.

Under the stars
you were born.
You have always been there
Even during times I could not stand nor bare

With a heart you influenced us.
With lungs you fought for us.
With a body you pushed us.
With a mind you were prosperous.

Under the stars
you were born.
A person who keeps me steady and calm.
I am grateful to call you mom.

The Days After...

I destroyed your heart and it wasn't on purpose.

I destroyed your love and all you ever wanted to do
was give it to me.

I destroyed the very essence that had given us a chance.

I wanted to succumb to your body but my trauma wouldn't allow it.

I wanted to fall into you completely and wrap you tight around me.

The trauma was like an infestation plaguing my mind and heart and
wouldn't let go.

I destroyed you from ever loving me again.

That trauma no longer exists, yet I still crave to be yours.

I hate that I love you.

I don't want to be a friend.

I don't want to be your lover I want to be yours forever, but forever
is no longer an
            OPTION.

That Lead to This

Today I said hello but it wasn't simple.

Today I told you I was sorry.

When my soul burned in the fire that's all I ever wanted to do.

Staring at Death in the eyes, you would never know
how much I loved you.

How I've always loved you, and that realization was scarier than
Death.

I love you and I always have.

I love you and I always will.

Today I said a word I've been trying to say and you said it back,
        HELLO.

Senescent Temple

I should treat my body like a temple.
I should treat it with care and respect.
Men objectify my personality, and I let them.
Turning me into their desires,
fulfilling both of our deepest fantasies.

I should treat my body like a temple,
but the hormones of my structure
push at the close, and I awaken
wanting them; all men surrounding me.
Then I feel emotionally unavailable.

I should treat my body like a temple.
I would have a partner instead of unlimited
possibilities and ending tragedies.
Maybe then I would feel happy *actually*
instead of immeasurable regret.

I should've treated my body like a temple
because I'm devastated to be alone.
I'm trapped in the limbo between hoe
and love, and I know men would see me
as only one. Then choose me as only
        ONE.

Triskelion

I had a dream about you.
At first, I was shocked
to see you, but then I
forgave you.
Most importantly, I forgave
myself.

You had thought this gesture
was an opening, but with a
smile, I said no. With ease,
I banished you and walked
away with
        PEACE.

Whisper Is a Shadow

Whisper is
the creep in the crevice
of my ear.
The silent dream rattling
my cords to scream.

Whisper is
the crisp winter's breeze
that told me to kneel
on his knees until
he was satisfied.

Whisper is
the everlasting, daunting
darkness manipulating
and manifesting vivid
hallucinations.

Whisper is
the brother-fucker who
exists in plane sight but is
"hidden" by the unjustified
bastards.

Whisper never apologized
for his psychotic, toxic behavior.
Instead, he told me time
and time again how it was my
fault.

Whisper is
a liar, a sinner, and a joke.
He was educated on stealing
love and hope: manipulations
upon conversations that never
            happened.

Whisper is
a dramatic, seductive storyteller
leading you on to believe his injustice.
The crash-course blond dignified
his lie upon lies in his multiverse
            of truths.

Whisper is
a Shadow, floating in a sea of stars,
watching my beautiful traumas
bloom into
            HAPPINESS.

Survivor's Night

The Death that speaks my name

      smells like fruit and chocolate.

I know it seeks the soul of my body,

      but it can't find what's lost.

It seeks the warm blood running

      through my veins.

The blood that speaks the words,

      "Death has come again."

My body was riddled with shame

      of an event that took my name.

So, Death could not take

      what was already stolen.

Now, Death seeks the light I crave

      but I am hollow like a fall stump.

I am as empty as a haunted house.

Blood and chocolate spreads

      through my nostrils.

My body is pushing past the limits,

      shackles and all.

Road to Love

I told him I was sorry.
I forgave him: my ex.
I made amends to his character.

I disrespected him
on an emotional level.
He couldn't trust me.

Sending him this letter
had allowed me to surrender
and truly let go.

> "Ah my Goddess, what's this
> peculiar sensation?"

My heart had felt a surge
of love and light. I cried.
I wasn't aware how big
my heart was until it expanded.

I didn't know that area was so gray.
So kept in the dark, refusing refuge
and salvation. I cried so hard.
For once, I'm healing

from the troubled, wicked past.
I'm accepting what is possible
and forgiving what was once
impossible.

I'm falling in love with the character
I'm creating because it's the love
of honesty and harmonic chivalry:
the love I'm manifesting to

LOVE
        ME
            TOO.

Exonerate Your Soul

Bubble, bubble, puff, puff.
Close your eyes, inhale, and feel
the energy shift from within.
Exhale and release the trauma
blocks weighing you down.

Bubble, bubble, puff, puff.
Forgive your shadow-self,
everyone who hurt you, including
yourself. Unlearn subconscious
programming to heal from
self-victimization.

Bubble, bubble, puff, puff.
You don't have to fight
to survive anymore. Exonerate
yourself, allow love to flourish,
and embrace your soul. Then,
open your eyes and
        LIVE.

Dancing with a Familiar Stranger

Dance a duet in the rain
with your soul and let it
sing.

Feel as your aura expands
and flows gracefully
like a sheet of satin velvet.

Let your soul find love
in the notes of each song.

Feel the grace of the melody
in the mercy of the rhyme.

Feel the movement vibrate
to the frequency of your shine;

   Your
    POWER.

Whiskey with a *Twist*

I took asylum in your reincarnation.
I felt your warmth
engage with my essence.

I took refuge in your eyes.
Their everlasting power
ravaged my vessel.

My elastic sheath
took every hypnotic gaze,
and my skin transformed.

Lips softened like
medium-rare steak.
You were my whiskey:
        the *twist* of my soul.

Be Proud Beneath <u>Your</u> Beautiful

It's quite okay. It wasn't your time back then.

You weren't as sure or positive but now you are.
You look at life with detail and precision.
You know your value and your worth.
You're ready for this next step towards graduation.
Be proud of where you are.

> You've grown to be kind, giving, and loving but you
> could've been worse.
> You could've been in a ditch and sipping coffee somewhere
> in heaven,
> in a pub eating peanuts ordering twelve shots of tequila.
> You could've been pumping your stomach at three a.m.
> before work.
> You could've been in an alley left for dead or worse.
>
> You did it right and now you're here.

Be proud of where you came from.

> Surviving to thrive is worth a celebration.
> Soon you'll be twenty-eight and to think, you didn't know
> you'd make it to eight-teen.
> We made it to another ten years.
> A decade, a milestone has passed.

Be Proud. You're in a better place.

> You have a home, a family, friends, and support system.
> You're surrounded by love you've allowed to let love you.
> You were always so hard on yourself.
> It's nice to see you've let it go and let in love.

Be proud. Don't think of all the things that haven't or won't happen.

> Is it a possibility? Sure, but you haven't made a choice
> because the conditions are still constructing so why are you
> making a choice on a pseudo reality?
> The same conversation you've had with yourself isn't your
> friend.
> It's a tall-tale-lie of infinitive recycling.
> End the cycle to set your mind free of each lie because the
> links to your shackles are still three feet long.

Be proud. You started at twelve.

> Each link held a lie you told yourself, but you've allowed
> yourself to expose your heart.
> In doing so, you allowed your soul to dive deeper into the
> depths of

> > What you are.

> > Why you are.

> > How you are.

> > Where you are.

> > When you are.

> > Who you are.

> > **Be PROUD.**

I Had a Dream

I had a dream
> where books surrounded
> my body.

> Each one different
> and telling the origin
> of the writer's journey.

> Like the autobiography
> of their soul.

> Each page detailed
> with precision and focus
> like composers of opera.

I had a dream
> that took my breath
> and felt surreal.

> Frames of strangers
> hanged across the walls,
> along with quotes and lines too.

> I felt an odd sense of happiness
> and I didn't want it to stop.

> I felt a sense of belonging,
> hope, and purpose.

I had a dream
> where a blue piano
> sang a symphony
> of broken rhymes.

Voltaire sat idly by
with a quill dripping ink.

Face blank
as if frozen in time.

Five thousand books craving
to be opened and read,
and a dozen more waiting
to be bound.

I had a dream
 and I can't wait
 to be conscious.

Unblocking the Self[3]

Looking back, I see that I was the creator
of my own violent darkness. I granted
negativity access into my heart and mind.
Mercury and Venus were always in retrograde
playing with my life like tug-of-war.

When my sisters were born, I became
a whisper in the hallways. My father
or step-mother would ask one question,

    "Did you eat?"

When I was sent back to my mother's,
I would react. I never understood why
my family thought I wanted attention
when I cut. When I bled slightly and silently,
surrendering to the sinister voice inside.

I could've been healed with a hug
instead of being interrogated. Now,
I see the attention I begged for manifested
a twisted reflection I had lived for twenty-two
    years.

That mirror was self-imprisonment. Lost
in a fabricated image between reality
and survival. Anxiety, depression, PTSD...
Tangled in the lies and lives of innocent selfish
greed in the search for love.

---

3   Content warning: early childhood sexual assault

At age six, when my sister was born,
I was molested. This age is significant
as it was the date of age my existence ceased.
I attempted to speak the horrific truth,

but every time I tried, the words got stuck
in my throat. After a few drinks, my mother
would laugh loudly in my abuser's home.
Home, in my bed is where I wanted to be.

However, a drunken mother's state waved me
away and I would shake in terror until morning.
I felt abandoned.
Though both of my parents are alive, there were
moments in life, I felt like an orphan.

I stopped trusting love.
                    It tortured me.
            Manipulated me.
                    Molested me.
            Raped me.
                    Abandoned me.

I'm a fucked up person healing like a puzzle,
only you can't see all of my pieces.
They're under development as I'm learning to unlearn all of my
toxic traits and behaviors I've carried for twenty-two years.
I'm educating myself to be intimate and kind by starting to unblock
        mySELF.

Awake

I've woken up.
I've embraced love.
Running through the house,
opening all of the windows
to let in the beautiful
wondrous light.

I've woken up
to the excitement
of a new dream. The
thrill of an actuality
of a perception
that is real.

I have woken up
and I feel grateful
to be alive. I feel humble
to be connected to the
frequency and heartbeat
of the universe.

I have woken up
to live the manifestations
I have created. I breathe
air, I drink water, I walk
on soil, I bathe in the sun's rays
feeding my spirit with love.

I woke up
and I feel with calm certainty,
I will be okay. I know this road
will have its own challenges
but I continue with grace
and a huge smile on my face.

I woke up
and I healed my relationship
with my mother. I love her truly
and I forgive her. I allowed her
to love me back and we hugged.
I could feel our souls intertwine.

I am awake
to receive the affection
and give it back to the world.
To attune to the moon and let
her know,
> *"Thank you for guiding*
> *my soul back to me."*

I am awake
to attract the beauty of independence.
To reestablish the colors I see
with my eyes to not be color blind
to darkness. I am no longer resistant
to the change and the
      TRUTH.

Sailing the Hurricane

a poem within a poem

Thunder claps, lightning, and rain.
The roaring dark clouds hold the closure
of **haunted** memories and mourn.

One by one each **droplet** dives
into a puddle like sheet music
creating a beautiful song.

Finding solace in the melody
of the piano keys.
The rhythm sings to my heart

in a sweet **everlasting** echo
of wonder.
I close my eyes to see my heart
undress to the world it once feared.

My soul danced to the harmony,
of the crashing waves. My energy
transformed the sadness into **love**.

I had never felt such a tsunami
of acceptance **for** myself. Before,
I'd let zephyrs push me back.

Now, I calmly exhale the howling gales
that the world tried to use and control
to contain **my** sexuality.

My **existence** is the evolution
of the aftermath, of my once dying soul.
The thrashing reapers of my past,

the blood-lust bastards, I didn't
allow them **to** triumph. At the eye
of the storm, I chose me.

The counter-clockwise seductive
spiral can no longer hurt me,
for I have chosen to **sail** forward.

My body, like a vessel, has traveled
nautical miles and has not,
will not sink to **the** depths

for the fear of the prejudice.
I found my value in the acapella
of the **hurricane** after years of being

a captive prisoner to the sadist cyclone.
Blaming myself for denying my truth.
A hypocrite **to** my own words.

Searching for **a** reason to be good enough.
However, the reality of the mirror
was to glance, not stare and live forever

in a twisted reflection of pseudo tempting
truth. Reviving in the moonlight, navigating
in the sea of wishes to a **bright** and steady

Tomorrow.

Now read the bold words from beginning to end

Homecoming

At the end of a battle, we see who stayed by our side.
We see their value and feel their love radiate across our body.
In the beginning it felt hot and awkward.
A sudden shift inside my chest.
They may have come from different backgrounds, but they came
together and waited patiently for my return.

Allow Love to Be <u>Your</u> Light

Hold
yourself
gently, embracing
who you are without
inspection.
Without fear
of external appearance.
Fall in love with the
internal character
you are creating and
exonerate your soul of
cenesthopathy to feel the
magnitude of your love.
Don't chase a beacon; become
your own lighthouse. Be proud
of all your layers. Silence the
shadows and become a constellation.

Kimono

I am a poet

who uncovers

the truth

through your eyes

and will help you

discover

that your

prison of flesh

is just a robe.

Requiem

I once was in a place
between losing my mind
and finding my soul.
So, I learned and understood
            patience.

The tricks my mind plagued
me with, mistook bad days
for a bad life. I could've been better.
Instead, I lived my life feeling anxious
            and depressed.

Life could've been easier, but
then the person in the reflection
would be a *different* person. He
wouldn't understand value and
anticipation or humiliation.

His life would be a privileged
dream full of suits, money, and deceit.
The unlimited fear of transformation.
The hunger to fight the war for a crisp,
fresh breath of air.

He wouldn't know.

He wouldn't be able to endure
the complexities of our lively soul.
He wouldn't be able to witness
the rapturous emotions of our body.

He would run.

He wouldn't be able to handle
the visits from the shadows
         that creep in each corner.
He wouldn't know how hard it was
to lie to everyone and say with a smile,

    "I'm okay."

But I never gave him the opportunity
to prove my evidence as justifiable.
I never wore his shoes, so my emotions

            are misplaced.
         I chose a destiny to breathe
               and find peace.

I am the experiment gone wrong.
The genetic mutation between lost
and found. I chopped off my fearful
roots to soar into cosmic dream clouds
and
         EVOLVE.

Veteran of the Void

The "call of the void," an expression
for a hidden death wish. It comes once
in a while banging my brain to make
an impulsive, reckless, death-defying
decision.

However, there comes a point in life
where you are no longer compelled
to write about the sinister,
seductive, and comfortable force
that used to control every action
both voluntary and involuntary.

> I'm a veteran of the void,
> an inanimate concept
> with a malicious heart
> and a malevolent mind.

What's important is that it no longer
has control.
It can no longer make verdicts,
and it can no longer pick up
> the knife.

> Its famous history became irrelevant
> and the critique hidden in the shadows
> grew scarce.

> I never got my license because
> I was terrified I would swerve
> on purpose.
> I had been so out of focus
> that my lens never gave attention
> to the needle on the compass.

Once I paid attention to the signs,
I was surrounded by hope and by magic.
Surrounded by the endless possibilities
of direction because the moment I accepted
love, a legion of opportunities stood before me.

Looking for a reason to fight, but all the villains
in my life, including myself have been unmasked.
I knew there would be a time when I would be happy,
but never did I expect for it to come *so* soon.

A place I never thought I would be is in this
state of mind where I am ME completely.
Here I stand six feet above ground
standing over the grave of the void.

> "I gave you my power and today,
> I take it ALL back."

> Restoring the power I gave you.
> Reclaiming the life I offered you.

Blind battles and vexed voices still try to penetrate
my borders, but I dismiss their vengeful conquest.
It's not my fight.
I hung up the towel and picked up a cup of lavender and chamomile
tea to sit outside and enjoy the fresh, sweet, calm air.
Enjoy the creative tones and vibrant lively pictures:
        a natural scenic **euphoria**.

Takeoff

Taking flight into a new life reminds me of
the darkness that wouldn't let go.

Its barbed wires coiled around my freedom.
Always fighting to stay alive.

Do you know what it's like to live without
being a hostage to your own mind?

The
runway
is clear for takeoff. Closing my eyes,
the plane ascends. Ten. Nine. Eight. Seven.
Six. The door opens. Five. Four. Three.
Two.
One...

A new adventure,
a life I never had the option
of living, awaits.
Here I go, taking a
/ /
/

L
EA
P

Hello Gentle Spirit,

This is the final *Checkpoint*.

How are you?

Healing is an important process we venture into at some point in our lives. I had to heal. There was too much going on and I needed to understand why.

Be kind, gentle spirit because there's only one of you and there's no one else like you.

Be strong, gentle spirit because you only have so many chances to change the outcome.

Be determined, gentle spirit because you don't want to miss your moment.

Be confident, gentle spirit because you are capable of surpassing "potential."

Closing

Thank you for reading my book. Thank you for learning and discovering my truths in all of its forms.

My abuela always tells me to grab the bull by its horns and push as hard as you can, which is a saying about life: When you have a dream, fight like hell to fulfill the dream. Don't wait for a breakthrough. Get up with every fiber of your being and push.

I could've ended up in many places, but I didn't. My family could be visiting my grave, but instead I get to physically see them proud of me. When I was eighteen, I didn't think I'd make it to graduation, but I did. Then I moved on to bigger and greater things.

The universe is quite interesting. We never truly know where we'll end up and that's okay. Welcome the unknown WITH open arms and take a leap of faith (whatever that is).

Outro

With this pen I will...

> Detail every word
> > like the notes
> > on sheet music in concert.

> Bewitch your mind
> > with a side of meters
> > and delicious cryptic rhymes.

> Save a life
> > like the first pen
> > I held *did too.*

> Fill every page
> > with voice, passion,
> > and silent precision.

> Take responsibility,
> > for the craft I create
> > is powerful.

> Make sure the lines
> > are refined and define
> > the truth of my soul.

> Leave a mark amongst
> > the twisted, fixated trees
> > and broken songful leaves.

Devote my life
        to bring clarity to darkened minds,
        and support those who are
        lonely and disconnected.
    Share the colorful
        and wicked stories
        of my journey.

With this pen I will…

Acknowledgments

CLI, thank you for selecting me to be a part of a community where like-minded individuals come together for the same goal of publishing their soul.

Community Literature Initiative Team:

Hiram Sims, thank you for creating a safe space where poets fulfill their dreams.

Andres Sanchez, my first instructor and mentor, thank you for teaching me to honor all of my emotions.

Alex Petunia, thank you for your patience, encouragement, peace, and serenity each week.

Karo Skaa, thank you for your creative passion and helping guide the creative flow.

My Family:

Roxanne Acosta, my mother and biggest critic, thank you for never giving up on me, even when I did.

Chrysinthia Bean, my older sister and friend, thank you for supporting me through this rollercoaster of a journey.

Salina Maynez, my person and partner in crime, thank you for staying by my side, helping me through the darkness, and helping me believe in my own magic.

Dink Santana-Lombardo, my lover (best friend), thank you for loving me unconditionally, listening to poetry for two hours, and giving me feedback to be a better writer.

Veronica Sedillo, my best friend, thank you for supporting and pushing me to be the best version of myself, and creating life-long memories.

Rebecca Vazquez-Navarrete, my dear friend, thank you for helping me get into the CLI Program and fulfill my biggest dream.

Resources

If you or someone you know is experiencing suicidal ideation, please reach out to the following hotlines:

National Suicide and Crisis Lifeline	988
National Suicide and Crisis Lifeline (for Deaf and Hard of Hearing)	For TTY Users, use your preferred relay service or dial 711 then 988
Crisis Text Line	Text HOME to 741741
Substance Abuse and Mental Health Services Administration Helpline	1(800) 622-4357
National Grad Crisis Line (Graduate Students)	1(877) 472-3457
National Suicide Prevention Lifeline	1(800) 273-8255
National Alliance on Mental Illness (NAMI) Helpline	1(800) 950-6264 Email: info@nami.org

If you or someone you know is/has been a victim of sexual assault and/or domestic violence, please reach out to the following hotlines:

Domestic Violence and Intimate Partner Violence

National Domestic Violence Hotline	1(800) 799-8233
Love is Respect—National Teen Dating Abuse Hotline	1(866) 331-9474 Text: 22522
StrongHearts Native Helpline	1(844) 762-8483
Pathways to Safety International	1(833) 723-3833 Email: crisis@ pathwaystosafety.org
Gay, Lesbian, Bisexual, and Transgender National Hotline	1(888) 843-4564 Youth Talkline: 1(800) 246-7743 Senior Helpline: 1(888) 234-7243 Email: help@LGBTholtine.org
Women's Law	Email: https://hotline. womenslaw.org/

Sexual Assault

Rape, Abuse, and Incest National Network (RAINN)— National Sexual Assault Hotline	1(800) 656-4673
Department of Defense (DOD) Safe Helpline for Sexual Assault	1(877) 995-5247

Children, Youth, and Teenagers

National Center for Missing and Exploited Children (NCMEC)	1(800) 843-5678 Cyber Tipline: https://www.missingkids.com/gethelpnow/cybertipline
ChildHelp National Child Abuse Hotline	1(800) 422-4453
Boystwon USA—Your Life Your Voice Helpline	1(800) 448-3000 Text VOICE to 20121

If you or someone else is facing a life-threatening situation, please call 911.

A Note from the Publisher

Riot of Roses Publishing House was founded in 2021 specifically to amplify the stories of historically silenced voices.

Xicana owned. Mujerista focused. For the people.

We publish books to heal and liberate.

Read our rebellion. To learn more, visit:
www.riotofrosespublishinghouse.com

RIOT OF ROSES
PUBLISHING HOUSE

SEJATNGA
UNCEDED TONGVA TERRITORY
SOUTH WHITTIER, CALIFORNIA

www.ingramcontent.com/pod-product-compliance
Lightning Source LLC
Chambersburg PA
CBHW021716120626
46545CB00004B/1587